THE LAST UNEXPLORED PLACE ON EARTH

THE LAST UNEXPLORED PLACE ON EARTH

Investigating the Ocean Floor with Alvin the Submersible

ALY BROWN

FEIWEL AND FRIENDS

NEW YORK

A Feiwel and Friends Book
An imprint of Macmillan Publishing Group, LLC
120 Broadway, New York, NY 10271 • mackids.com

Our books may be purchased in bulk for promotional, educational, or
business use. Please contact your local bookseller or the Macmillan
Corporate and Premium Sales Department at (800) 221-7945 ext. 5442
or by email at MacmillanSpecialMarkets@macmillan.com.

Library of Congress Control Number: 2023018573

First edition, 2023
Book design by Julia Bianchi
Feiwel and Friends logo designed by Filomena Tuosto
Printed in the United States by Berryville Graphics,
Fairfield, Pennsylvania

ISBN 978-1-250-81668-9
10 9 8 7 6 5 4 3 2 1

*To my amazing family for believing in me always.
And for every kid with a wondrous sense of
curiosity and adventure.
Go discover!*

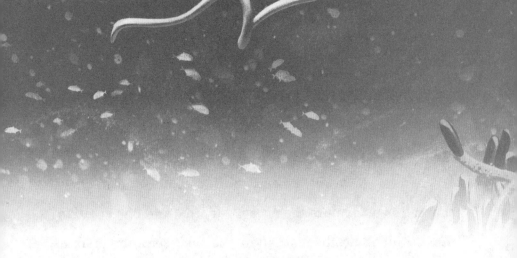

INTRODUCTION

No human has ever set foot here. There are creepy creatures with glowing tentacles and cruel fangs waiting to close around their next meal. It's where monsters sneak past seemingly harmless plants that might eat them whole and smoke billows from mutated rock formations.

No, it's not an alien planet, but it might as well be. In fact, we know more about the surface of Mars than we do about this place.

The depths of the ocean.

We have explored the far reaches of the globe, from the top of Mount Everest to Badwater Basin—a stretch of land 282 feet below sea level. For most of our time on this planet, however, the ocean has been a huge mystery.

Playing in the waves at the beach can make for a day of fun. But it's incredible to think that the meeting of water and sand is where two worlds collide.

Scientists have only recently built the kind of technology that helps us explore the ocean's depths, and one creation stands out above the rest: *Alvin*, the deep-sea submersible.

You're probably wondering what *Alvin* is. And no, it has nothing to do with a singing chipmunk. *Alvin* is a deep-sea vessel that can carry three people more than 4 miles below the water's surface.

ALVIN BEGINS ITS DESCENT TO THE BOTTOM OF THE OCEAN. (PHOTO BY GAVIN EPPARD, TAKEN MAY 21, 2006, EXPEDITION TO THE DEEP SLOPE/NOAA/OER)

That's pretty neat, but why does it matter? Why would anyone spend all the time and money it took to create *Alvin*? Beyond satisfying our curiosity or snapping neat pics, why would scientists go through the trouble?

It wasn't just for bragging rights, sea star selfies, or even the chance to break records . . . No, *Alvin* has been part of many important missions that have given researchers new information about the environment, how humans impact Earth, and even life itself—making scientists rethink how and where life could exist! For more than 50 years, *Alvin* has been adventuring in the deep blue. From capturing footage of the *Titanic*'s watery graveyard to revealing a part of the seafloor that was once unknown to scientists, the little vessel has uncovered a treasure trove of information after ages of human wondering.

But *Alvin* is more than just a hunk of metal. As *Alvin* pilot Bruce Strickrott has said, the submersible changes the life of everyone who's stepped aboard for a deep-sea dive.

"A lot of people look at the sub, and they see a machine—a cool machine—and they see cool people doing cool things with a cool machine, but there's a bigger story there," he

said. "In calling *Alvin, Alvin,* they imbued it with life . . .
I've watched people change critically."

Take a dive into the wonders of *Alvin*'s world and see
for yourself what lies beneath.

CHIEF PILOT BRUCE STRICKROTT AND ELECTRONICS TECHNICIAN SEAN McPEAK WORK ON *ALVIN* NEAR THE RESEARCH VESSEL *ATLANTIS.* (GULF OF ALASKA 2004. NOAA OFFICE OF OCEAN EXPLORATION)

CHAPTER 1

First, There Was Allyn

Allyn Vine ran through a puddle, clutching a fistful of cables and ignoring the chill of icy water that soaked through his socks. He couldn't wait to get home to examine the treasure he'd found near the Garrettsville Telephone Company on Main Street. The people who worked there had the delightful habit of tossing scrap telephone parts into a junk pile behind the building. And Allyn loved to rummage through the mess of tangled wires to find things worth saving.

Once back on Park Avenue, he darted up the porch

steps to his home and flung open the door. A welcoming fire crackled in the hearth, and he was tempted to sit by it and dry off, but his latest project called to him. That last bit of insulated wire from the junk pile was just what he needed to finish his radio.

Al loved building things and figuring out how they worked. His hobby might have seemed strange to other kids his age, but he would later credit the days he spent diving through junk piles, fishing for wires to make his creations hum with life, for helping to fuel a passion for invention.

He didn't need directions or fancy kits, and later as an adult, he said, "Too many engineers are designing from catalogs, while not enough are doing innovative work. This doesn't . . . inspire creativity."

Allyn's own creativity and ingenuity followed him as he grew up in the 1920s in Garrettsville, Ohio—where he was "fortunate in having a pleasant and instructive family and exceedingly good teachers in school."

FINDING A LOVE OF THE OCEAN

So how did a kid from Ohio, who grew up far from salty shores, decide to explore the ocean? His interest in geology, or the study of Earth, first launched that voyage.

After his telephone wire–collecting days, Allyn went off to nearby Hiram College and then to graduate school at Lehigh University, in Pennsylvania. It was there that one professor of geophysics—Professor Maurice Ewing, a.k.a. "Doc"—saw Al's talent and brought him under his wing. Doc was one of many scientists in the 1930s to realize that the study of geology had hit a wall—the majority of Earth's terrain was underwater, and there was little known about the bottom of the ocean. The next frontier for geosciences lay beneath the salty waves.

MAKING A NAME FOR THEMSELVES

In 1936, Doc won $2,000 in grant money from the Geological Society of America to take geosciences below sea level. With that money, Doc completed deep-water geophysical work with Woods Hole Oceanographic Institution

(WHOI)—a nonprofit group of scientists and engineers dedicated to ocean research and education. From 1937 to 1939, for two weeks at the end of each summer, Doc, Al, and a handful of other students set sail on a ship named *Atlantis*, with a mission to study the sediment at the bottom of the ocean.

Sediment is stuff that settles at the bottom of a liquid. In the case of the ocean, this can be the mud, sand, and other material resting on the floor. Allyn realized it also offered an important clue about Earth's history.

What Doc and Allyn found while measuring sediment velocities was that there was a surprisingly thin layer of sediments only 100 to 200 million years old (not several billion as expected). Sediment study would later play a significant role in supporting theories that Earth's continents had moved over time. But we'll get to that later!

They also spent this time taking photos of the seafloor and working on something called *reflection seismology*, which involves setting off explosives to send elastic waves into the earth. The way the waves reflected off different properties in the layers of the ground and sent that information back to

FIRE IN THE HOLE!

ALLYN also conducted a lot of his studies on land.

To research the earth under the surface, scientists place explosives into holes in the ground—called *shot holes*. The sound waves created from the explosions travel through Earth, reflecting differently depending on the density changes between rock and soil. Those waves are then recorded and studied to better understand what lies below.

This practice, Al said, wasn't always appreciated.

"One had to learn a certain amount of politics because you tended to drill your shot holes at the edge of the highway," Allyn said, chuckling. "So if the highwaymen came along, you said you thought you were on the man's property, and if a farmer came along, you said you thought you were on the highway. And then after the dynamite blew up, why, then you folded your tent and left as quickly as you could."

receivers helped them learn about the makeup of the planet's subsurface.

Even though Allyn and the other scientists were scraping up some answers from the bottom of the ocean, they were just scratching the surface of many deep-sea mysteries.

THE CALL FOR SUBMARINE EXPERTS

Allyn went on two more expeditions with Doc on the *Atlantis* and enjoyed them so much that, after completing his master's degree, he decided to work full-time for WHOI. Unfortunately, worldwide turmoil would alter his plans.

By 1941, World War II was already raging, and the US Navy needed help improving anti-submarine warfare—which basically means they were looking for, tracking, and sometimes destroying enemy submarines. With massive funding coming in from the navy, WHOI dove into wartime research.

Al's new job involved measuring and recording the speed of sound under the water. He took an instrument called a

bathythermograph—just BT for short—that looked kind of like a diving torpedo toy you might play with in a swimming pool. The BT was used to measure the temperature layers of the ocean. The researchers would attach a line to the BT and drop it off the side of the research

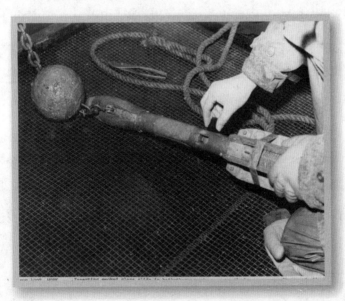

A BATHYTHERMOGRAPH, WITH A RESEARCHER INSERTING A SMOKED-GLASS
SLIDE INTO THE HOUSING. (PHOTO BY J. OLSON, NOAA CENTRAL LIBRARY
HISTORICAL FISHERIES COLLECTION, 1960)

ship. As it plummeted through the water, a tiny needle inside scratched a line on a piece of glass that marked the temperature in relation to the depth of the water. This was important information because sound travels at different speeds in different temperatures, and knowing where the temperature changed could help submarines hide from enemy sonar.

The focus for the United States soon went from anti-submarine to pro-submarine, and Al was a leading force in that shift. He improved the accuracy of the BT, modified it so that it could be mounted on submarines, and added display features to help the divers inside understand how their sub's sound was spreading through the water at different depths.

The navy later said Al's work with the BT contributed to "the savings of untold numbers of lives, and millions of dollars in ships and equipment."

Something else incredibly important that came out of these experiences? The friendships Al formed in the science community and with submarine operators. Even after the war ended in 1945, he continued working with other scientists and officials studying the ocean.

As the years wore on, though, they came to realize that

they needed better research tools. Submarines existed, yes, but they couldn't go *that* deep, and they didn't have windows or means for bringing back research samples.

In 1956, Al went to a symposium, or a meeting, put on by the National Academy of Sciences National Research Council in Washington, DC, to talk about better ways to study the ocean.

Allyn suggested that the best way to understand it was to take the plunge and explore the ocean in person. At the symposium, participants agreed to create a national program that would help build submersibles capable of taking people to great depths of the ocean.

And so the idea for a deep-sea research submersible was born.

IT DIDN'T HAPPEN OVERNIGHT

Building a machine that could sink deep into the ocean with people inside would take time, testing, money, and teamwork.

Al and others at WHOI requested bids to build a small

submersible capable of carrying three people to a depth of 6,000 feet. Putting out a bid is kind of like announcing to a bunch of different people and companies, "Hey, we want someone to complete a job. Who can do it well, and who can do it for the best price?"

The electronics division of General Mills—yes, the company that makes Cheerios—then said, "We can do this for $498,500!" and the company won the contract. While it might seem weird, General Mills used to make a lot more than cereal back then, and one of the company's engineers, Harold "Bud" Froelich, developed the vessel.

"This was in the days when General Mills was in business without boundaries, [that] was sort of the philosophy at General Mills," Bud explained.

When it came to paying for the submersible, the US Navy stepped in with money from the Office of Naval Research. The navy was willing to pay the bill for the new submersible because—much like during World War II—the government knew that a vehicle that could study enemy equipment and submarines would come in handy.

At last, work began!

One important feature of the submersible's design was

ALVIN FACTS

PART of what makes it so difficult to explore the bottom of the ocean is that there is a lot of PRESSURE under all that water. Without special equipment, anyone who dives deeper than 130 feet would be crushed. But *Alvin* was specially designed to withstand that pressure, protecting the passengers inside from getting smushed.

One way to illustrate this is with Styrofoam cups.

Styrofoam is great for keeping drinks hot, because of its air pockets. But deep in the ocean, the pressure squeezes out the air, leaving behind a mini cup.

The Alvin Group has welcomed decorated cups from classrooms and other groups across the nation. All of the cups are inserted into nylon pantyhose and stored in a compartment outside of *Alvin*'s sphere—a place that will feel the pressure. The force of that pressure on the cups makes them shrink! And the kids get to see their decorated cups in miniature form.

Another fun Styrofoam object to shrink? Wig holders. Talk about some shrunken heads!

the giant metal ball, called a *personal sphere* or *pressure hull*, where humans could sit inside. A hull is the watertight enclosure of a ship.

Steel and welding companies were hired to take 6-foot-diameter steel plates and shape them into multiple hemispheres that would later go through a series of stress tests before a final design could be approved. Scientists and mechanics tested these spheres often to the point of destruction.

"We had tried to think of almost every conceivable situation that might imperil human life, and devised ways to avoid such crises," Al said, adding that the design called for the metal sphere to detach from the rest of the submersible during emergencies. "In that way, the crew could escape if, say, the sub's arm or other projection became entangled in debris on the bottom."

Through many tests and designs—sometimes failures, arguments, and rebuilds—the size and shape of the submersible changed over time. And the little contraption the engineers had unofficially been calling the *Seapup* got a new name, *Alvin*, in honor of the driving force behind its creation: Allyn Vine.

WHO MAKES
EXPLORATION POSSIBLE?

WHOI does—at least from the driver's seat. Woods Hole Oceanographic Institution (WHOI) is a nonprofit organization in Cape Cod, Massachusetts. It's dedicated to marine research, engineering, and higher education. The institution was formed in 1930 with a goal of understanding the ocean's role in the changing global environment. WHOI is responsible for overseeing *Alvin*'s operations.

HOW IS THE US NAVY INVOLVED?

Technically, the US Navy owns *Alvin* and has used it throughout the years for things like studying the best ways to defeat enemy submarines.

WHO PAYS FOR THE ADVENTURES?

In addition to private donors, the National Science Foundation (NSF) helps pay for many science exploration adventures. The NSF is a government agency created to promote the progress of science. To secure funding, scientists have to write proposals (see page 110), which aren't always accepted. Scientists need to be good writers, too!

As Bob Houtman, of NSF's Division of Ocean Sciences, explained, "The successful partnership between NSF, the Navy, and WHOI ensures that researchers will continue to have direct access to the deep ocean for the next generation of scientists and scientific challenges."

CHAPTER 2

The Birth of *Alvin*

A long time had passed since that young up-and-coming geology student had dreamed of bigger and better ways to explore the sea. Finally, that dream became a reality.

On June 5, 1964, the US Navy's brass band played in full uniform as flags waved and officials led *Alvin*'s christening, which is the ceremonial launching of a new vessel. The ceremony saw men and women in formal attire come out to celebrate the creation of *Alvin*.

Al Bud (the General Mills engineer) and pilot Bill Rainnie made the very first ceremonial dive with *Alvin*. The little submersible, attached to a line, dipped into the water and plunged 70 feet deep. This first dive was largely a celebratory event, since *Alvin* didn't have a support ship handy to venture into the ocean, and it still needed to get its sea legs.

After a few more practice runs, on August 4, 1964, it was finally time for *Alvin* to take its very first untethered free dive. While it was a cautious adventure, only going to a depth of 35 feet, the dive was also an exciting success.

THE TESTING OF ALVIN, SUMMER 1964. (PHOTO COURTESY OF WOODS HOLE OCEANOGRAPHIC INSTITUTION ARCHIVES © WOODS HOLE OCEANOGRAPHIC INSTITUTION)

By 1965, *Alvin* had a brand-new support tender constructed from a pair of surplus navy pontoons called *Lulu* (named after Allyn's mom), and the sub voyaged to the Bahamas to help test the navy's underwater listening equipment known as ARTEMIS. That equipment was built to track enemy submarines.

A larger vessel that's used to support smaller boats is called a *tender*. *Alvin* has had several tenders in its lifetime—first *Lulu*, then *Atlantis II*, and now R/V *Atlantis*.

To study this equipment, pilots Bill Rainnie and Marvin McCamis took *Alvin* to its location at the Tongue of the Ocean—a deep-water basin in the Bahamas along the coast of Andros Island and surrounded by the Great Bahama Bank—a carbonate bank to the east, west, and south. Photos taken from above show a strip of dark blue in the middle of shallower turquoise-colored water.

Tethered to *Lulu*, Alvin went down to 7,500 feet for 12 hours—a trip that proved its hull was safe and sound.

ALVIN FACTS

To date, *Alvin* has had over 5,000 dives and spent over 35,000 hours submerged, with an average dive time of seven hours. The vessel helps support research for those who study biology, geology, chemistry, and engineering. It's also used for training new pilots and scientists. To this day, it's America's deepest-diving and longest-serving research sub. In August 2022, Alvin successfully completed a certification test to dive to 21,325 feet (or about 4 miles!).

Alvin is used by various scientific teams to study the ocean for different reasons—whether they're biologists looking for creatures or geologists studying rock formations. That said, the little sub holds only three people—one pilot and two science observers. Back in the day, there used to be a pilot, a copilot, and one science observer, but this was eventually changed to allow two science observers aboard at once. The scientists who are lucky enough to go on a deep-sea dive need to get pretty far out into the ocean before taking the plunge. So members of the Alvin Group take a research ship filled with supplies, the scientists, and *Alvin* far into the ocean.

Finally, on July 20, 1965, the pilots took *Alvin* on an untethered dive to 6,000 feet, which proved to the navy that the submersible could operate at test depth. This earned navy certification for the sub, and *Alvin* officially became the world's deepest-diving research vessel.

Since the Office of Naval Research owns *Alvin*, it has to pass Navy Sea Systems Command certification in order to operate. The sub can only dive based on the certification it receives. The navy conducts regular surveys and audits. The Alvin Group will often get letters detailing the things it needs to do to keep its certification.

An example is making sure all of the life-support systems in *Alvin* are maintained. When it comes to *Alvin*, the operations team has to do a lot of paperwork, too—meticulous inspection records must be kept!

CHAPTER 3

Explosive Discoveries

One year later in another part of the world and flying high above *Alvin*'s watery domain, a US B-52 bomber plane was carrying a full load of hydrogen bombs and running low on gas. But there was yet another war going on—the Cold War—and the crew wasn't about to land in the foreign territory of Spain with an arsenal of nuclear weapons aboard just to fuel up.

In order to keep the B-52 in the sky, a KC-135 Stratotanker with spare gas was sent to help. The two planes met in the air, and the plan was for the B-52 to fly in behind the tanker, as it extended a long tube (called a *boom*) to the plane and transferred the fuel. At high speeds and altitudes, with two planes trying to line up perfectly for the exchange, it's an understatement to call it dangerous.

But it was also a pretty common practice for refueling military aircraft—these planes guzzle a lot of gas as they zip through the sky at top speeds of nearly 600 miles per hour.

A BOEING B-52 BEING REFUELED BY A BOEING KC-135. (PHOTO BY US AIR FORCE)

"There is a procedure they have in refueling where if the boom operator feels that you're getting too close and it's a dangerous situation, he will call, 'Break away, break away, break away,'" recalled Major Larry G. Messinger, who had been aboard the B-52 that day, January 17, 1966. "There was no call for a break away, so we didn't see anything dangerous about the situation. But all of a sudden, all hell seemed to break loose."

The B-52 collided with the KC-135 Stratotanker's boom, which tore open the tanker and ignited the fuel. Fire raced up the boom to the storage tanks above, creating an explosion that lit up the sky.

All four of the KC-135's crew members died immediately. The B-52 lost its left wing, and out of its seven crew members, only Larry and three others escaped with parachutes, while the four hydrogen bombs the B-52 once carried fell toward the Spanish farming and fishing settlement of Palomares. Had those nuclear weapons been armed, they could have killed everyone living in southern Spain. Fortunately, the bombs' detonating systems weren't activated, and no one on the ground was killed when they fell.

That didn't mean they didn't cause their fair share of damage. Material in two of the bombs exploded on impact and scattered radioactive plutonium throughout Palomares's fields. An estimated 1,750 tons of soil and vegetation across a 1-square-mile area had to be removed and shipped away for proper disposal. And even with those precautions, the danger of overexposure was very real for the people who lived there.

The US paid hundreds of thousands of dollars to those who reported injuries because of the disaster.

LOSING PRECIOUS CARGO

The impact was devastating. Not only had lives been endangered and America had to pay for cleanup costs, but extremely dangerous weapons were missing. The US couldn't simply leave a nuclear weapon lying around for an enemy to find.

America's president at the time, Lyndon Johnson, ordered people to find the bombs.

Two were already accounted for because they had blown up on impact, causing the radioactive mess. Another was later found in a dry riverbed with little damage. But where was the fourth?

The mad dash to find it was now more pressing than ever as newspaper reports came out about the accident. Visitors fled the area, a huge upset for local businesses— tourists spend a lot of money! To calm nerves about pollution, US Ambassador Angier Biddle Duke and Manuel Fraga Iribarne, the Spanish minister of tourism, took a dip at nearby beaches in front of press photographers.

The question about the location of the last bomb lingered until an eyewitness report from a fisherman surfaced. He claimed he had watched the bombs fall from the sky and pointed investigators to a 1-mile area.

If the man was right, the last bomb had fallen into the Mediterranean Sea.

IN COMES *ALVIN* . . .

In February following the crash, *Alvin* boarded a US Air Force cargo aircraft at Otis Air Force Base and landed in Rota, Spain. Using a navy dock landing ship as its tender, *Alvin* and other navy vessels began combing the ocean floor off Spain for the lost bomb.

They spent the next month taking 19 dives in search of the missing weapon, until one day, on March 15, something fluttering in the water caught the *Alvin* crew's attention.

With Marvin McCamis piloting that day, they dove down a steep slope—scraping and bumping along the terrain—and discovered that the fluttering material was actually the missing bomb's parachute.

Finally!

With the bomb located at last, the navy attempted to retrieve it. But their troubles weren't over . . . During an attempt to attach lift lines, the bomb slid down a slope a few hundred feet into deeper water. It was far out of sight. Everyone sighed in disappointment. The search would have to begin again.

A TRICKY RETRIEVAL

It wasn't until April 2—after *Alvin*'s exhausted crew had spent seemingly endless days combing the area—that they relocated the hazardous weapon.

This time, they came prepared.

The search teams enlisted the help of a 15-foot, 2,000-pound experimental robot called CURV—which stands for "cable-controlled underwater recovery vehicle." CURV had to get an upgrade in order to dive deeper than its original 2,000-foot limit for the hydrogen bomb relocation mission. Once the upgrade was done, it was rushed from its navy lab in California to the search site.

LAUNCHING THE CURV-III REMOTELY OPERATED UNDERWATER VEHI-
CLE, SEPTEMBER 1973. (US NAVY)

The massive machine plunged through the water, bringing cameras with it for the crew to inspect the site. It had a single mechanical claw, and those controlling it could direct it to grab things. So imagine playing an arcade claw machine game, but the goal is to pick up a hydrogen bomb instead of a stuffed animal . . . No pressure.

CURV tangled itself on purpose around the parachute of the bomb while attaching its own lines, and on April 7, the crew wrenched the bomb back up to the surface.

Thanks to *Alvin*, the hydrogen bomb had been found and recovered!

CHAPTER 4

Not So Many Friends
in Low Places

While everyone was pretty excited about *Alvin's* recent navy certification and its success in finding the lost hydrogen bomb, Mother Nature sometimes had a different opinion of the little sub . . .

The team was out completing dives for both the navy and scientific research in the Bahamas in 1967 when something flashed by one of the viewports. Pilot Marvin McCamis would have ignored it had it not been for the strange sound coming from the hull. The three aboard exchanged nervous glances.

They were 2,000 feet below the surface, and something was definitely *not* right.

Marvin looked out the viewport again and saw what he thought was a boulder—until it darted away. Suddenly, a rasping noise exploded around them. Then copilot Val Wilson shouted, "We've been hit by a fish!"

The pilots looked out the thick porthole glass to catch a glimpse of a large, dark fin flitting past. They were hit again.

The hits kept coming, until—quite suddenly—they stopped. It was suspiciously still and quiet, except for the roar of the men's hammering hearts.

Blood clouded the water just outside the viewports. Water leaked into the sub's vital electrical circuit, causing a shrill alarm to sound.

Alvin headed to the surface.

When the support crew on the surface pulled them onto the deck, everyone gawked at the sub with their mouths hanging open. The three inside *Alvin* stepped out, wondering what the crew could be staring at. That's when they saw it. A swordfish was stuck to *Alvin*'s frame. During the attack, the fish had become entangled and rode with the vessel all the way to the surface. The animal's 1.5-foot sword had pierced a seam separating two pieces of the submersible's body.

ALVIN FACTS

WHILE *Alvin* takes the plunge, most of the scientists and crew members stay at the surface to offer technical support, kind of like the mission control center at NASA. This might mean monitoring the sub's position or guiding the pilot toward a target of interest. If something is off, the mission has to end, and they return to the surface.

Even though everyone agrees it's better to be safe than sorry, for those inside *Alvin*, an aborted mission is no fun, especially since it takes about two hours to reach maximum depth. As Susan Humphris, former chair of the WHOI Department of Geology and Geophysics, will tell you, it's quite the commute to work!

It takes time to sink because *Alvin*'s pilot has to allow certain amounts of water into the ballast tank, which is a sealed-off portion of the vessel that holds water. The more water allowed into the ballast, the deeper the submersible goes. So the pilot regulates the amount of water to start and stop diving. The vehicle also has steel weights that the pilot can jettison (release) into the water when it is necessary to go up or back to the surface altogether. If *Alvin* gets stuck at the bottom of the ocean, it can also jettison propellers and other equipment to tear itself free and bring the crew to safety.

After all that, the researchers can explore for about four hours—assuming everything goes well—and then it takes another couple of hours to return to the surface. A full day's work!

A SWORDFISH ATTACKS *ALVIN* IN 1967! (PHOTO COURTESY OF WHOI ARCHIVES © WOODS HOLE OCEANOGRAPHIC INSTITUTION)

The damage wasn't terrible, but the reality of how bad the situation could have been was finally understood. Swordfish have been known to attack and sink boats by piercing through the wood with their swords. Alvin isn't made of wood, but the fish still managed to stab two pieces of the sub's body before it was dragged to the surface.

The crew members knew they had been lucky. And in the end, at least they had a good dinner that night and an interesting story to tell!

DO YOU WANNA FIGHT?

As pilot Bruce Strickrott will tell you, that was only the first interesting sea critter encounter *Alvin* and its crew had. There have been many others. Strickrott loves to make voices for the creatures he sees, especially the ones that try to fight the submersible.

"They take a look at the lit-up thing, and the groupers, which are pretty territorial, come right to the window with their dorsal fins up," he said. "We're a threat. Some things run from threats; others stand up to fight."

Swordfish that attack *Alvin* sometimes lose their bills, offering a yummy snack for nearby crabs. On one dive near coral, a large swordfish whipped around the submersible. It was clearly making its point: *Get off my turf!* The crew watched with interest, hoping it wouldn't charge the viewports.

"I really didn't want to have to abort the dive for a scratched window made by some pissed-off fish," Strickrott said, laughing.

But then the fish disappeared. Suddenly, bits of coral began raining down on them. The angry swordfish had bit off a chunk of the coral and spat it at *Alvin*!

ALVIN FACTS

HOW do you breathe inside *Alvin*?

Alvin carries enough oxygen that three people could survive for three days, even though the submersible is never underwater that long. And, as WHOI scientist Susan Humphris noted, there's also a piece of equipment with a chemical that captures the carbon dioxide (CO_2) that people breathe out. This is very important because at certain concentrations, CO_2 can be harmful. Breathing in too much CO_2 can cause bad headaches, dizziness, decreased brain function, increased heart rate, loss of consciousness, coma, or even death.

Imagine three people breathing into a sphere together and none of the CO_2 they're breathing out can escape. That would get pretty concentrated!

Bruce has also seen sea lions much deeper than he thought they'd ever swim or a dumbo octopus gearing up to defend itself. He even looked out the viewport one day to see a massive eye staring right back at him. It was a Humboldt squid. These creatures are large predators that can grow up to 6 feet long and weigh over 100 pounds. The one that came to visit Bruce started to mess with the samples *Alvin* had collected in its collections basket.

A FEMALE OCTOPUS DOESN'T WANT TO LET GO OF *ALVIN*'S ARM. (PHOTO BY BRUCE STRICK-ROTT, COURTESY OF EXPEDITION TO THE DEEP SLOPE 2006, NOAA-OE)

Experiment

EVER wonder how mammals stay warm in the icy ocean? The answer is somewhat simple: blubber! This thick layer of fat insulates marine mammals. Try this "blubber glove" experiment to get a sense of how it works.

YOU'LL NEED:

3 large quart-sized plastic bags with a zipper
1 container of lard or shortening
heavy tape
2 bowls of icy water
2 rubber kitchen gloves

STEP 1: Put tons of the lard/shortening into two plastic bags. Spread it evenly throughout the bag so that you have a 1-inch-thick layer. Seal the bags.

STEP 2: Place the bags of lard together and tape three sides together, forming a "mitten." Then place that mitten into the third bag.

STEP 3: Put the rubber gloves on both hands. Then stick one of your hands into the lard mitten bag and dunk it into one of the ice water bowls.

STEP 4: Dunk your other hand into the other ice water bowl.

Notice a difference?

CHAPTER 5

Lost at Sea

O ther misadventures weren't so funny . . .

On a morning before the last dive of the season in 1968, *Alvin*'s crew darted about the deck of the *Lulu*, making sure things were in order. Ed Bland, Roger Weaver, and Paul Stimpson were scheduled to be *Alvin*'s pilot, copilot, and scientific observer (in that order).

While *Lulu* was the beloved boat that first brought *Alvin* to sea, the truth was . . . it was just a little thing built with leftover money after constructing and testing the submersible. Technically, *Lulu* was a registered motorboat with a neat job, but not a whole lot more.

ALVIN AND ITS ORIGINAL CATAMARAN SUPPORT SHIP, *LULU*, 1971. (OAR/NATIONAL UNDERSEA RESEARCH PROGRAM [NURP] VIA THE NOAA PHOTO LIBRARY)

And since there wasn't much room, the crew members had to go through an awkward procedure when getting *Alvin* into the water. *Alvin* had to sit in a cradle suspended by cables in between *Lulu*'s twin hulls. This allowed the crew to raise and lower the submersible into the water through a rectangular hole in the center, which was a task in itself! The pilot would stand on top of *Alvin* with the hatch open, while the other two divers for that day would climb inside with their lunches and whatever else they needed, like extra sweaters or socks. Then the pilot had to help guide the chief engineer as they lowered *Alvin* into the water. (Kind of like when someone gets out of a car to help shout directions to the driver who's trying to park in a tight space without hitting things.)

Not ideal, but that was how it was done at the time. So Roger and Paul climbed inside, while Ed stood on top of *Alvin*, offering directions.

Without warning, one of *Lulu*'s cables snapped— then another!

Ed jumped from *Alvin*'s top and clung to *Lulu*'s hull as the submersible fell more than 10 feet from the cradle into the ocean. Seawater quickly gushed into the open hatch, pinning Roger and Paul against the walls with incredible force. The submersible started to sink as more water plunged inside.

The next few seconds were critical. It was the amount of time it would take for *Alvin* to completely fill with water before plummeting to the bottom of the ocean with helpless victims inside. That time was also their saving grace. With air still trapped inside, *Alvin* popped back up to the surface.

When *Alvin* broke through the water, the alert crew chief, George Broderson, jumped into action, knowing the sub would soon fill up and sink for good. He grabbed Roger's arms and pulled, and Paul scrambled out behind, clinging to Roger's legs. Just in time, too. *Alvin* went back under, and this time—now filled completely with water—it plummeted to the bottom of the ocean, over 5,000 feet below.

They'd lost *Alvin*.

But the crew members weren't going to give up on the little sub. Thinking quickly, they began grabbing lawn chairs and pieces of metal that had been sitting on *Lulu's* deck and threw them overboard.

Why? As people who made a living looking for things underwater, they wanted large, visible objects that would help them know *Alvin* was nearby when they returned.

SEARCHING FOR *ALVIN*

The quest to find *Alvin* began immediately. Other ships went to the area where the crew knew the submersible had been lost. WHOI even rented another submersible, but no luck. Months passed.

It was a horrible loss for everyone who cared about *Alvin*. It seemed the vessel was gone for good.

It wasn't until the next year, when one of the navy's cameras snapped a photograph underwater, that hope resurfaced. There, sitting upright on the seafloor, was *Alvin* with its hatch still open, waiting to be found by its people.

"Months before this, during the long winter, I and many others at Woods Hole had written off the little sub in our minds," said Bob Ballard, WHOI marine geologist. He explained in his book *The Eternal Darkness* that the photo was just what they needed to inspire a rescue mission after a long period of hopelessness.

Now that *Alvin* had been found, the question became *how* they would get it back to the surface. It wasn't tethered to anything, and while *Alvin* was pretty small, as far as submarines are concerned, it was still really heavy and sitting at the bottom of the ocean.

TOGGLING BETWEEN RESCUE MISSION IDEAS

They had to come up with a plan for this one-of-a-kind rescue mission, and it would require help from a fellow sub.

Aluminaut was a bigger, clumsier vessel. The world's first aluminum submersible, made by the Reynolds Metals Company and sometimes hired for use by the navy, it would only prove useful for a total of six years—but at that moment, all eyes were on *Aluminaut*.

ALUMINAUT, A 51-FOOT-LONG, FIVE-PERSON SUB, MARCH 1972. (OAR/NATIONAL UNDERSEA RESEARCH PROGRAM [NURP])

The plan on paper seemed simple: *Aluminaut* would take a cable with a toggle bar at the end down to *Alvin* and put the toggle bar inside *Alvin*'s open hatch; then the surface crew would tow *Alvin* close to shore where it could be pulled out of the water.

The reality, however, was something different. *Aluminaut* dragged down the 7,000-foot reel of cable to *Alvin* as planned. But when the *Aluminaut* crew aboard tried to place the toggle inside *Alvin's* hatch, the underwater currents whipped it around. Twelve hours passed. The *Aluminaut's* power was running low, and the waves were getting too high to continue working. Disappointed, everyone returned to shore.

Later that month, they returned with renewed confidence and determination, and this time *Aluminaut's* mechanical arm flexed its skills to successfully drop the toggle into the hatch.

While the moment was a joyous accomplishment, they had another problem to solve. *Alvin* was filled with water, weighing thousands of pounds. So the crew towed it to shallow water off Martha's Vineyard, where a crane fished it out and placed it on a barge.

By the time the barge returned to Woods Hole, an anxious crowd had gathered on the dock to welcome *Alvin's* safe return nearly a year after being lost at sea.

Alvin couldn't resist contributing to science, even during its lost year. When recovered, the vessel taught us something valuable.

The crew's lunches left onboard before the submersible sank in 1968 were completely preserved. There were three bologna sandwiches, apples, and a thermos of broth. Other than being wet from seawater, the sandwiches looked and tasted—yes, the brave scientists even took a bite—like they would have tasted a year before. The apples, though a bit pickled from the salt, still had similar qualities to that of a fresh apple.

CLIFF WINGET HOLDING A SANDWICH FROM THE SALVAGED *ALVIN* IN SEPTEMBER 1969. WHAT? FIVE-YEAR RULE! (PHOTO COURTESY OF WHOI ARCHIVES © WOODS HOLE OCEANOGRAPHIC INSTITUTION)

Microbiologists Holger Jannasch and Carl Wirsen turned the discovery into research. We know that cold temperatures help preserve food—that's why we keep leftovers in the fridge—but these scientists soon realized the deep-ocean pressure also slowed down how quickly things decomposed. This discovery led to a series of new microbiology experiments.

Inspired by *Alvin*'s sandwiches, the scientists continued to document extremely slow rates of microbial decomposition in the deep ocean. They even designed new tools to collect more samples of bacteria at great depths and injected the seafloor with organic material to see how quickly bacteria would grow. Their work offered valuable scientific information about deep-sea food chains.

But perhaps the most relevant—and arguably most important—result of this discovery was data that supported the end of deep-sea dumping. See, people used to think that it was okay to take a bunch of mankind's trash and throw it in the ocean. Sink it, and forget about it, right? It would probably just decompose under all that water, they thought. But instead of degrading over time, it just sat at the bottom, causing long-term exposure and damage to the ecosystem.

Holger's research showed that since we're trying to get *rid* of pollutants, the bottom of the ocean—with its slow rate of microbial degradation—is clearly not the solution.

ALVIN GETS A REVIVAL

While those discoveries were useful, the deep-sea dive wasn't as helpful to *Alvin* itself. Sitting in the salty water for a year had corroded metal inside the vessel and left a layer of mineral deposits. And *Aluminaut*'s trick with the toggle bar might have helped bring Alvin back to the surface, but it also broke propellers and smashed holes in the fiberglass during the struggle. Plus, instruments inside *Alvin* had imploded from the pressure of the deep sea. Everything was a mess!

Even though the submersible was found and saved in late 1969, it would take two years to put it back into working order. And by the time *Alvin* was ready for adventure again, the little vessel would have a very special guest.

ALVIN FACTS

ALVIN has seven reversible thrusters—propellers facing sideways—that help it move backward, forward, up, and down. Two of the thrusters are used for turning. The sphere the crew sits inside is supported by a titanium frame, and special syntactic foam surrounds the giant ball—a feature that helps it float. *Alvin's* design allows the pilot to navigate the underwater world, hover, or even rest on the seafloor. Several LED lights help illuminate the dark water.

While syntactic foam might sound similar to Styrofoam, it's actually a combo of polymer mixed with preformed hollow spheres. These little spheres are usually made out of glass, ceramic, or even metal. *Alvin* needs this special material because syntactic foam is resistant to pressure and long-term exposure, which makes it great for subsea equipment.

CHAPTER 6

Lady Luck

It was Friday the 13th, and Ruth Turner was about to do something very unlucky.

Unlucky, that is, according to some old seafaring men. See, for a long time, it was considered bad luck to bring a lady on board a ship. But on August 13, 1971, Ruth, a professor at Harvard University and a malacologist (someone who studies shellfish), was about to put that superstition to the test and become the very first woman to deep-sea dive with *Alvin*.

On the day of the trip, she looked out the window in amazement. The deep sea filled her with wonder, but she remembered to take research notes. Allyn Vine was also aboard that day.

"I said to Allyn Vine, I said, 'Al, what's the date today?'" Ruth remembered. With a laugh, she impersonated his voice. "'What? Don't you know it's Friday the 13th, and we had the courage to take the first female down in this thing!'"

Ruth wasn't the type to take offense at Al's teasing, though. Known as a spunky, "tiny woman with a strong jaw and equally strong opinions," she was the type to play poker with the men and smuggle specimens onto airplanes in her underwear.

When asked if she had ever been scared while diving in *Alvin*, Ruth shook her head and immediately said, "Nope!"

"I figured the pilots wanted to come home just as much as I did," she said. "So if they weren't scared, why should I be scared?"

She was more concerned about what she'd discover.

CHIEF *ALVIN* PILOT RALPH HOLLIS (LEFT) AND RUTH TURNER (RIGHT) NEAR *ALVIN* ON R/V *LULU*, 1983. (PHOTO BY ANNE RABUSHKA © WOODS HOLE OCEANOGRAPHIC INSTITUTION)

Ruth had a mission to uncover more information about clams and shipworms. Since these creatures were known to destroy wooden ships and docks, Ruth wanted to study their life cycles. The information would help people create ways to control the damage the animals did.

Before diving with *Alvin*, Ruth had spent decades gathering specimens attached to cruise ships, but she wanted to know what lurked in the deepest part of the ocean. If a sandwich could be preserved down there, why not ancient shipwrecks?

A MICROSCOPIC VIEW OF A SHIPWORM BEING EXTRACTED FROM A BLOCK OF WOOD. (PHOTO BY ROBERT F. SISSON, COURTESY OF NOAA CENTRAL LIBRARY HISTORICAL FISHERIES COLLECTION)

CRAZY CRITTERS

IN the mid-1960s, scientists were able to answer the questions of seafaring folks who wanted to know why their sonar signals were sometimes off. The sonar would give a false read when tracking the depth of the ocean. Woods Hole biologists suspected something was intervening . . .

The theory was that dense layers of fish, or siphonophores, were tripping up the sonar when they made their nightly migration toward the surface. Using the cover of darkness, they could stay safe from predators while gobbling food in the upper layers of the sea.

So in 1967, scientists strapped a sonar device to *Alvin*, turned the lights off, and tiptoed 2,000 feet deep. When the equipment picked up something on the scope, they flipped the lights on. There, surrounding the vessel, were thousands of lantern fish.

The reason the fish were messing up the depth readers was because all of their tiny bodies swimming so closely together formed a massive wall that the sonar signals bounced off!

9/19/01 08:49

THOUSANDS OF LANTERN FISH SURROUND *ALVIN* DURING A DIVE INTO HUDSON CANYON. (IMAGE COURTESY OF DEEP EAST 2001, NOAA/OER)

While working with *Alvin*, Ruth used the submersible to sink a number of wooden planks to depths of 6,000 feet. About 100 days later, the boards came back in really bad shape. Unlike the bologna sandwiches that were preserved by the deep-sea pressure after being underwater, the wood crumbled apart when *Alvin*'s mechanical arm went to pick it up.

Humans have long known the damage shipworms could bring to docks and boats. The ancient Greeks even wrote about them. But didn't the creatures mainly pester man-made wood structures near the surface? Wasn't the deep sea a place of suspended animation? Why hadn't the planks survived 100 days when the sandwiches had gone almost a year with no change?

When picking apart the pieces of wood brought back to the surface, Ruth found what she'd been looking for—proof that a different species of deep-sea shipworm existed!

Ruth's theory was that these little critters had evolved to cope with the deep environment and used bacteria in their gills to help them digest the wood. The creatures were another interesting find, but they also upset marine archaeologists. If these mollusks ate wood, it would be pretty difficult to find well-preserved ancient shipwrecks!

Ruth's woodworm discovery was significant—and so was the trip she took with *Alvin* as the first female passenger. But as she later said during an interview for the Harvard Community Resources, she didn't really care so much about being the *first*.

"I just really didn't give it a whole lot of thought," she said. "I was too busy doing my work."

Ruth was 57 when she made that historic dive inside *Alvin*, and she went on to become one of Harvard University's first female tenured professors. She continued scuba diving and lecturing at the university until the last decade of her life.

Before she died in 2000, Ruth had become a world-renowned biologist. She was known to tell students, "Do what sets you on fire!"

The fire that was Ruth Turner sparked a blaze in many women who followed after her.

ALVIN FACTS

WHAT'S it like diving with *Alvin*?

Amazing, incredible, life-changing, yes. But it's also cold! And the deeper you

BRUCE STRICKROTT (LEFT) AND SUSAN HUMPHRIS (RIGHT) INSIDE THE *ALVIN* SPHERE, 2014. (PHOTO BY CHRIS LINDER © WOODS HOLE OCEANOGRAPHIC INSTITUTION)

go, the colder it gets. Bring extra socks, sweaters, and hats. Water vapor that condenses on the inside of the vessel sometimes trickles down your back. WHOI scientist Susan Humphris said the *Alvin* crew has been known to play a joke on newbies by pretending the sub's sprung a leak.

"When you're stuck in a bowl together for eight or nine hours, you'd better have a good sense of humor," Susan said.

One tricky thing to sort out before heading off is the issue of the bathroom—in that there isn't one. (But if you really have to pee, there's always a bottle on board!) Susan said when she is diving, she dehydrates the night before, so she is less likely to need to pee while diving.

Sitting in a cold fishbowl with no bathroom access for hours might sound pretty terrible, but for adventurous scientists, it's still a dream come true.

Pilot Bruce Strickrott described the sights, sounds, and sensations of exploring with *Alvin*.

"You can hear the ambient white noise of the ocean, but if there are whales or dolphins nearby, you can hear them, too," he explained. "We go to some mind-blowingly amazing places—you're in a canyon at the bottom of the ocean, at volcanoes—and you see these creatures that live in it all. Then there are massive walls that dwarf Half Dome and rocks bigger than houses, perched on ledges. There's a place in the Mid-Atlantic that looks like Tim Burton designed it."

"Once you're down there, you're so busy, you don't think about anything else," Susan said. "Many times, when you go down you have no idea what you're going to find. The opportunity for discovery is always at the back of your mind."

CHAPTER 7

On a FAMOUS Mission

Whether searching for bombs or discovering new ship-eating worms, *Alvin* and its crew were always eager to take off on a new adventure. Whether they were always *ready* was another matter, because in 1974, the little submersible was asked to go to places—and depths—it had never gone before.

Seeing the potential of submersibles for research, geologists from America and France decided that now was the time to explore a controversial theory: that Earth's continents were once much closer together, perhaps were even a single landmass, and had drifted apart from one another over millions of years. One of the best places to look for the evidence they needed would be the Mid-Atlantic Ridge—the world's longest underwater mountain range. If their theory was right, and the continents were moving, they would find evidence that new seafloor was being created there.

To get a visual of what the Mid-Atlantic Ridge looks like, imagine draining the ocean and taking a picture of our planet from space; we'd see a long mountain line running down the center of the region between North/South America and Africa/Europe.

America and France teamed up for Project FAMOUS (short for French-American Mid-Ocean Undersea Study). Naturally, *Alvin* was assigned to help.

There was just one *itty-bitty* problem . . .

The Mid-Atlantic Ridge was about 9,000 to 10,000 feet deep, and *Alvin* couldn't go that deep. The little sub was only certified to dive to 6,000 feet. *Alvin* needed an upgrade.

The submersible received a new pressure sphere— remember, that's the metal ball that the divers sit inside.

This time, instead of steel, they decided to go with a metal called *titanium*. Titanium is nearly twice as strong as steel—a new sphere made out of that stuff meant it could be the same weight and size it was before, but it could withstand *twice* the pressure. Thanks to this improvement, Alvin was able to dive way down to 12,000 feet—the little sub was more than ready to go!

DSV *ALVIN* BEING REFITTED WITH A NEW TITANIUM PERSONNEL SPHERE SO IT COULD JOIN PROJECT FAMOUS IN 1974. (OFFICE OF NAVAL RESEARCH, US NAVY)

SO WHAT EXACTLY WAS *ALVIN* GOING TO PROVE?

We'll need to backtrack a bit to help answer that question. Remember how scientists were trying to prove that the continents had moved apart from one another? That concept was called the continental drift theory. For a long time, it was the laughingstock of the scientific community. But meteorologist and geophysicist Alfred Wegener—the guy who came up with the first comprehensive theory on the topic in 1912—was on to something.

He noticed that the continents of the planet looked something like a puzzle with pieces that had been pulled apart. South America seemed like it would fit nicely into the curve of Africa, for example. Alfred even pointed out that there were similar fossils and matching rock formations found in Brazil and West Africa.

He proposed the idea that about 250 million years ago all

PROFESSOR ALFRED WEGENER, CIRCA 1924–1930. (PHOTOGRAPHER UNKNOWN)

modern continents had once been part of a supercontinent he called Pangaea, from the ancient Greek word meaning "all lands."

But other geologists made fun of Alfred's idea and also of Alfred himself. A lot. In fact, it became so bad that older scientists warned the younger ones coming into the field to never even mention the theory, saying it would ruin their careers. *Ouch*.

A huge problem for Alfred was that he never found the proof. He had a theory, yes, but it largely lacked an explanation. It failed to provide a "how"—*how*, then, did the continents drift? Scientists at the time wanted Alfred to explain what kind of force could actually move an entire continent. Certainly not the tides! Without that answer, his "evidence" just seemed like a bunch of unrelated facts smashed together in an attempt to prove a wild idea.

While he didn't quite have that piece of the puzzle, Alfred stood by his theory until he died in 1930, which was unfortunately before the scientific community had a "my bad" moment and decided to revisit the concept of moving continents.

WHY DID SCIENTISTS GIVE ALFRED WEGENER'S WILD IDEA ANOTHER CHANCE?

Beginning in the 1950s, the technology for seafloor mapping had improved. Experts were able to confirm that the Mid-Atlantic Ridge existed, even though people used to believe that the ocean floor was basically flat. Deep-sea dredging operations in the area even brought back volcanic rock, suggesting that magma rose through cracks in the earth's surface and hardened. Could it be that underwater volcanoes were causing these mountains . . . and *possibly* the movement of land?

During the 1960s, the seismographs installed around the world to detect enemy nuclear tests at the time of the Cold War uncovered something else for science. Even though they were looking for enemy activity, they discovered that the natural earthquakes were all happening in the same places. Not only that, but based on the speed of seismic waves in certain regions, it suggested there was a soft layer within Earth's mantle, providing a place where the continents could drift apart.

A huge breakthrough came in 1963, when magnetic maps of the Indian Ocean showed a strange pattern of magnetic properties—the patterns on the seafloor from opposite sides of the Mid-Atlantic Ridge were a *perfect* match.

See, Earth is basically a giant magnet. Its inner core is made of solid iron and nickel, which are both magnetic materials. The movement of these elements creates Earth's magnetic field. In the past, this field has occasionally reversed: North becomes south, and south becomes north. When lava erupts, it cools and locks in the magnetic field at the time. With continued spreading, that lava moves farther and farther away from the axis, but it retains its magnetic orientation. So you end up with these zebra stripes of magnetic normal and reverse periods.

Then in 1966, a geologist named Patrick Hurley gave a talk at the History of the Earth's Crust Symposium that helped change even more scientific minds. He explained how he had used radiometric dating—a technology that could calculate how old geologic materials were by measuring their radioactive elements—to show that rocks from Brazil and Africa were not just similar, but actually the *exact* same age.

There were too many new facts to ignore. The old debate around Alfred's theory had been revived, and the theory of plate tectonics was born. This newer theory offered the "how" that Alfred's continental drift theory lacked. With plate tectonics, it was believed Earth's outermost layer is made up of large plates, which lie on top of a molten layer of rock. Due to transferring heat and movement in the molten layer, the plates move relative to each other, creating mountains and rifts—which are kind of like canyons or tears in the land.

Keep in mind, however, that plate tectonics was still just another theory, meaning that smart people had a smart idea about how something worked, but it still needed more proof.

Experiment

ESSENTIALLY, Earth's crust is broken into pieces, or tectonic plates. It has seven large plates, six or seven medium-sized plates, and several small ones. The plates sit on top of the mantle, which is the next layer of Earth. The mantle is made up of both solid and molten rock called *magma*.

To get a visual of how the plates move when the magma rises, try this fun experiment with the help of an adult.

YOU'LL NEED: one Styrofoam plate and a frying pan filled with corn syrup. During this experiment, pretend the corn syrup is like Earth's molten rock mantle, and the pieces of the Styrofoam plate are Earth's tectonic plates.

STEP 1: Cut the ridges off the plate, so that you only have the flat portion.

STEP 2: Draw lines on the plate to create about 4–5 "puzzle pieces."

STEP 3: Cut carefully along the lines you've drawn so that you can still arrange the pieces into one whole plate (again, like a puzzle).

STEP 4: Place the pieces, arranged as one whole plate, into a frying pan filled with corn syrup.

STEP 5: Slowly heat the corn syrup and watch as the bubbles begin to move the plate pieces away from one another. This is like watching the magma rise through Earth's plates to push them apart.

DOWN, DOWN TO THE
VERY BOTTOM!

On June 6, 1974, with its new sphere in place, *Alvin* boarded the *Lulu*, which was towed by WHOI's new research ship named *Knorr*. Together, they set sail for the Mid-Atlantic Ridge alongside two French-owned vessels that transported their own submersibles, *Cyana* and *Archimede*. This kind of coordinated deep-diving mission had never been carried out before. And even though humans had already set foot on the moon in the summer of 1969, Project FAMOUS was the first time they had been to a mid-ocean ridge.

This expedition was also another significant milestone for female scientists. According to scientific rosters for *Knorr*, of the 38 people who embarked on the various FAMOUS voyages, 8 of them were women. The group of women who managed to secure their place for Project FAMOUS had diverse roles and backgrounds. Even though they didn't dive in *Alvin*, their jobs included logging data and samples, surveying, dredging, and analyzing materials.

Kathryn D. Sullivan was in her first year of graduate school at Dalhousie University in Nova Scotia when she was asked to support Project FAMOUS. She recalled that one reason the women couldn't dive in *Alvin* was because it was believed *Lulu* didn't have the facilities to support them—a.k.a. a girls' bathroom. ("As if any of our home bathrooms were devoted to females . . . ," she scoffed.)

She said there was a chalk line drawn along the *Knorr*'s deck—a line she was told to stay behind, since women were "a distraction on the fantail." On one in-port visit, a captain's wife told her she was to serve appetizers during a reception with officials from France and America.

"Needless to say, I didn't take too kindly to this suggestion," Kathryn said. "Mustering what few shreds of civility I could, I tersely told her that I planned to be representing my university in the laboratory, and other waitresses would have to be found. WHOI scientist Bill Bryan came to my aid, peeling me off the ceiling and deflecting any further requests for members of the scientific party to be cross-assigned into the mess division."

On her four cruises, however, Kathryn said she felt accepted as a member of the scientific party and that the experience toughened her up.

"The pressures, difficulties, personal challenges now all sit in a broader perspective for all of us," Sullivan continued, "and we are glad we got to be a part of such a pivotal expedition."

This pivotal expedition took *Alvin* and crew along a 5,000-foot ridge and into a rift valley that looked like an underwater Grand Canyon. It was like entering another world within our world! Seasoned *Alvin* diver and scientist Bob Ballard, along with his team, could see with their very own eyes the scenic beauty lying beneath the ocean.

And then they saw it—the neatest discovery of all . . .

There at the seafloor, they saw fresh-looking lava formations unlike any seen on land. The deep-sea pressure and icy water had created the unusual shapes. And many of these formations showed evidence of destruction due to fault activity. The science observers would soon discover that they had found the longest chain of underwater volcanoes where lava welling up through fissures, cooling and hardening over and over again, had helped to create the mountainous terrain and rifts. Could this be a key discovery in proving that the seafloor was indeed spreading?

Alvin and the other two submersibles returned lots of times to continue studying the area. The three were often in the water at the same time, and the crews had to use advanced navigational techniques to keep track of each sub. Altogether, *Alvin* and friends made 44 dives. During that time, they brought back 3,000 pounds of rock samples, plus water and sediment specimens. Along the way, the scientists also took thousands of photos.

Thanks to this monumental discovery and the study of magnetic stripes, scientists formed a groundbreaking hypothesis about how the spreading could be occurring. Through magnetic studies of sediments, they determined that the plates were moving at a rate of one inch per year—about as fast as fingernails grow. Given that scientists were looking at movement taking place over 250 million years, the spreading rate over time added up for the continents to be in their current positions. Someone owed Alfred Wegener an apology!

CHAPTER 8

Smoke in the Ocean?

No sooner had scientists solved one mystery than another arose. Geochemists had found rocks with chemical traces of hot-water circulation.

Something down deep below was causing this . . .

The Southtow and Pleiades expeditions in the early '70s pinpointed a region to explore. So at the beginning of 1977, Bob Ballard and *Alvin*, along with a team of 30 geologists, geochemists, and geophysicists, set out on a new special mission: the Galapagos Hydrothermal Expedition. They would go to study the Galapagos Rift, which was about 400 miles west of Ecuador, to search for hot springs. Bob, who had been part of Project FAMOUS, was asked to be co-scientist for the trip to the Galapagos because he had experience running submersible programs in complex volcanic terrains.

Since they didn't want to waste precious *Alvin* diving time searching the vast ocean for something worth looking at, scientists sent ANGUS, a towed camera, to image the seafloor. ANGUS snapped a pic every 10 seconds as it was towed a few meters above the bottom and brought back thousands of overlapping images. The robot had a temperature sensor as well.

Then something happened.

The research ship, *Knorr*, received a signal from ANGUS—a spike in temp. For a short period, ANGUS had picked up a brush of warm water. Since they had synched up the robot's timing for both photos and temperature data, the crew would be able to figure out where the pictures had been taken at the exact moment it recorded a flush of heat.

But reviewing the photos was not as simple as scrolling through a smartphone album. They had to be developed—a process that starts with removing the roll of negatives from the camera and processing them in a batch of perfectly mixed chemicals, then hanging them to dry for several hours. Once they'd finished with this lengthy process, and had sorted through hundreds of photographs, they saw something that made the wait worthwhile.

There—in what was supposed to be a land void of any life in the deep, dark ocean—were hundreds of clam and mussel shells. How could this be? The deep, cold water with no light whatsoever couldn't possibly support life!

LARGE CLAMS LIVING WHERE NO LIFE SHOULD BE ABLE TO... SEEN THROUGH *ALVIN'S* PORTHOLE. (PHOTO COURTESY OF WOODS HOLE OCEANOGRAPHIC INSTITUTION ARCHIVES © WOODS HOLE OCEANOGRAPHIC INSTITUTION)

After ANGUS caught pictures of the clam shells, the Alvin Group went down for a closer look. Pilot Jack Donnelly brought researchers Jack Corliss and Jerry van Andel to the place where ANGUS had spotted the creatures.

But they found more than clams. Shimmering clouds of warm water rose from cracks in the lava and from unusual mounds of orange sediment that were teeming with creatures—clams measuring over a foot in length, crabs, fish, and lifeforms they'd never seen before. There were weird wormlike tubes sticking out of nearby rocks.

CLOSE-UP OF A TUBEWORM TAKEN APRIL 2, 2012. (PHOTO: NOAA OKEANOS EXPLORER PROGRAM, GULF OF MEXICO 2012 EXPEDITION.)

Thanks to the time Bob had spent along the Mid-Atlantic Ridge, he was expecting another lifeless landscape waiting for him on the ocean floor. Instead, he was blown away. There were similar fresh lava flows here, but the Galapagos Rift was an oasis of spectacular creatures.

"When my turn came again to dive...I was overwhelmed," Bob continued. "Never before or ever since have I seen so much strange and exotic life."

What they had discovered were hydrothermal vents!

AN ACTIVE HYDROTHERMAL VENT CHIMNEY SPEWING OUT HYDROTHERMAL FLUIDS. (PHOTO COURTESY OF SUBMARINE RING OF FIRE 2006 EXPLORATION, NOAA VENTS PROGRAM)

CRAZY CRITTERS

ALVIN'S dives around the world resulted in discoveries on all levels. Many times, the trips led to the discovery of new creatures. Scientists found new species of mussels, whelks, limpets, anemones, worms, snails, lobsters, crabs, and brittle stars, among others. A vent site was later named the "Rose Garden" when scientists found massive 8-foot tubeworms with red tips. It was discovered that this place without light thrived with life.

A BLACK SMOKER, DISCOVERED TWO YEARS AFTER THE FIRST HYDROTHERMAL VENTS WERE FOUND IN THE GALAPAGOS RIFT IN 1977, IS ANOTHER TYPE OF HYDROTHERMAL VENT THAT CAN HOST A COMMUNITY OF GIANT RED TUBEWORMS AND HUNDREDS OF SQUAT LOBSTERS, AS SEEN HERE. (PHOTO: UNIVERSITY OF WASHINGTON; NOAA/OAR/OER)

With a hydrothermal vent, cold seawater filters down through cracks into the lava beneath the surface. As it does this, it gets heated up from the volcanic activity below and rises back to the surface, expelling clouds of hot chemical-rich water that often looks like smoke. When the materials cool, they solidify, forming chimney-like structures made of copper, iron, and zinc sulfide.

In total, they found five sites in the area that supported the life of these bizarre deep-sea animals. Even though the critters were clearly thriving around the hydrothermal vents, they couldn't quite explain how they were surviving way down there. Where could they possibly be getting their food from?

The bewildered scientists were eager to find out. *Alvin* grabbed some things to study and secured them in the specimen basket.

DSV *ALVIN* SETS A LANDER BASKET WITH TUBE CORES ON THE BOTTOM OF THE OCEAN. (PHOTO: OAR/NATIONAL UNDER-SEA RESEARCH PROGRAM [NURP])

Experiment

CAN'T visit the bottom of the ocean? No problem! With some help, try this experiment to replicate a hydrothermal vent.

YOU'LL NEED:

1 large glass container (like a Mason jar)
1 small glass bottle
food coloring
string
hot and cold water.

STEP 1: Tie a piece of string around the neck of the small glass bottle.

STEP 2: Fill the Mason jar with cold water.

STEP 3: Fill the small glass bottle with hot water and some food coloring of your choice.

STEP 4: Holding the string, lower the small glass bottle into the Mason jar, making sure to keep the bottle upright.

What happens? That hot water should "billow" out of the glass bottle, and since you've used food dye, you can watch it. Looks like a hydrothermal vent. Pretty neat!

That night, one of the chemists opened water samples, and a rotten stench swept through the entire research ship. It was like someone had hidden hard-boiled Easter eggs a little too well and forgotten about them. (Or like someone had eaten them and their stomach was taking it out on the crew trapped in the same air space.) Either way, it was horrible. But they also realized this was yet another clue.

The rotten-egg smell was hydrogen sulfide. Deep fissures in the rift were allowing cold seawater to go into the seafloor, where it reacted with hot rock. As a consequence, the chemical makeup of that seawater changed, and sulfates in the water were reduced to hydrogen sulfide. And the clams and tubeworms had bacteria inside them that helped them metabolize this hydrogen sulfide. They were performing a process called *chemosynthesis*—when organisms use energy released by chemical reactions.

Before this discovery, it was believed that much of the life on our planet depended upon light, a.k.a. photosynthesis. With photosynthesis, plants convert sunlight into glucose (food) in the chlorophyll, and then that food is broken down by cellular respiration to release energy. Then other creatures either eat the plants, or they eat other creatures who have eaten plants, or both.

But this little oasis along the Galapagos Rift was a deep-sea ecosystem dependent on chemosynthesis.

This discovery challenged everything we knew about where life could begin and thrive. The Galapagos Hydrothermal Expeditions made the scientific community realize that this life-giving process could take place at the bottom of the ocean.

ANOTHER HYDROTHERMAL DISCOVERY

Many scientists were inspired by the discovery of the vents, including marine geochemist Dr. Susan Humphris, who had studied rocks from vent sites in the 1970s before taking her first dive in 1986.

"We didn't even know (the vents) existed until 1977," she said. "On our own Earth, we didn't even know that was going on—imagine what could be found on other planets . . ."

Before this dive, she'd been studying rock samples already collected while working to complete her PhD. She was interested in these hydrothermal vents and their geochemical characteristics. Her supervisor at the time gave her some helpful tips, reminding her that once she was down in the sub, she needed to record an explanation of what she was seeing. He warned her not to fill her tape with things like, "Oh, that's amazing!" because she'd have no clue what that meant later on.

Once beneath the surface, the otherworldly sights nearly made her do just that. She was totally awestruck.

"We were crawling around on the bottom of the Atlantic Ocean, and all of a sudden, I saw the most incredible sight of this huge chimney covered in shrimp!" Susan said. "And I started going, 'Wow! This is amazing! I can't believe this!' Then all of a sudden, this little voice got into my ear, and I thought, 'Oh, no, that's not what I'm supposed to say.'"

Immediately, she began voicing her eyewitness experience with scientific details that would make her supervisor proud.

CRAZY CRITTERS

WHEN scientists discovered hydrothermal vents, they also uncovered a strange world of never-before-seen creatures, including an interesting species of shrimp that appeared to have an eye on their backs.

Biologist Dr. Cindy Van Dover studied them and discovered that the shrimp have two flaps of light-sensitive tissue running along their backs. Their "eyes" are actually infrared sensors that help them sense high temperatures of the direct venting as they need to be close to the chimneys for their food.

Since the vents churn hot water, Cindy believed that the shrimp might have developed a remote sensor "so they don't get cooked."

Working to study these shrimp also helped scientists make another discovery. They placed a camera near the smokers, then turned off *Alvin*'s lights. The pictures they captured showed that the vents themselves let off a certain amount of light.

Susan and the crew had stumbled upon the biggest hydrothermal vent site yet discovered in the Atlantic. It proved to be one of the largest mineral deposits in the ocean. And there were different organisms at the vents in the Atlantic compared to those in the Pacific.

"Because it was the first discovery in the Atlantic, and it was my first dive, we were all super excited at finding it," Susan recalled. "It was really dramatic."

"Life is in many forms in the ocean that we wouldn't know about if we just stuck to land," she continued. "Ever since the discovery of the vents, a new animal has been found about every 10 days. The amount we don't know about our own planet is huge."

Susan explained that the vents are made of copper and iron sulfides and that many of the mineral deposits we mine on land for those metals originally formed at the bottom of the ocean.

For Susan—who grew up in England before joining the MIT-WHOI graduate studies program—the discovery was a dream come true. She went on to contribute to over 100 publications on hydrothermal vents. She has been a

huge advocate of education, bringing many undergradu-
ate students and K–12 teachers to sea.

She also reported another extraordinary observation:
the change in attitude toward female scientists. In the
1970s, some of the crew so
strongly believed that having a woman aboard was
bad luck that they wouldn't
even talk to her.

"Nowadays, you go out
and sometimes more than
half of the scientific crew
is female," Susan said. "So
there's been a huge change
over the last 50 years around
the acceptance of women
being at sea."

SUSAN HUMPHRIS INSIDE *ALVIN*'S SAIL, 2013.
(PHOTO BY TOM KLEINDINST © WOODS HOLE
OCEANOGRAPHIC INSTITUTION)

CHAPTER 9

Sinking with the Unsinkable

After years of oceanographic discovery, one scientist had his sights set on a treasure hunt.

Way before *Alvin*'s time—and two years before Allyn Vine was even born—an "unsinkable" ship called the *Titanic* sank in 1912, after colliding with an iceberg.

The jagged chunk of ice had left a 300-foot gash along the ship's side, and by the time the captain inspected the damaged area, five compartments had already filled with seawater. To make matters worse, the officials at the time had been so cocky that the *Titanic* couldn't sink that they didn't have enough lifeboats. In about three hours, the massive vessel brought most of the souls aboard down with it to a watery grave. Of the 2,223 people who set sail on its first and only voyage, 1,517 died in the icy Atlantic waters off the coast of Newfoundland. The disaster quickly became known around the world.

To this day, over 100 years later, the *Titanic*'s sinking remains a well-known tragedy. This tale of a luxury liner that met its demise despite its state-of-the-art design has been the inspiration for many movies and books. In fact, one well-known film director, James Cameron—who's behind movies like *The Terminator* and *Avatar*—said that the inspiration to make *Titanic* in 1997 first came from a deep dive he took in a submersible.

Perhaps the only truly unsinkable part of the *Titanic* was its ability to captivate the world. Because generations later, the desire to find the ship remained as strong as ever, especially for Bob Ballard—the WHOI marine geologist who helped discover hydrothermal vents in 1977.

Somewhere deep in the stormy, cold waters of the Atlantic Ocean, the massive *Titanic* waited to be discovered.

And since so many scientists, engineers, marine historians, and treasure hunters were eager to uncover its resting place, the race was on to find it.

The problem for Bob, though, was that this quest to find the ship didn't exactly serve a scientific purpose. When asking for money to use *Alvin* for research, the WHOI group had to come up with something better than, "Because we want to." Every other trip had served some kind of purpose, right? So how would this benefit science?

Still, Bob wanted to find the sunken unsinkable ship. Other groups had gone out to search for the *Titanic*, and the thought of someone else finding it only fueled the tension for him.

Bob had been working on two remotely operated vehicles (ROVs) named *Argo* and *Jason*, and by 1984, they were ready for sea trials. The little robots were tethered to the research vessel, so humans could control them from the surface, instead of going down into the water. They both had cameras, and *Jason* even had a mechanical arm, just like *Alvin*. The navy wanted the *Argo/Jason* system to grab footage of sunken ships and submarines like the USS *Thresher*, which was lost in 1963. The reason the navy was looking at these vessels remained confidential, but it was funding missions, so off they went.

DEPLOYING THE ROV *JASON*, SEPTEMBER 2008. (PHOTO BY JEREMY POTTER; NOAA/OAR/OER)

But then, a glimmer of hope! Finding the *Titanic* went from being somewhat of a joke—a pipe dream—to a race against other countries. (It was kind of like how America rushed to set foot on the moon before anyone else in 1969.) The navy had sent *Argo* to explore the wreck site of the USS *Scorpion*, but, finally in 1985, it offered an awesome incentive to Bob: Once you're done with this survey, you can take the remaining navy-funded time to use *Argo* and the research ship *Knorr* to do whatever you want.

Bob had three weeks.

He and the team worked around the clock to map the USS *Scorpion* area in late August 1985, and they managed to bring back the information the navy wanted in only four days. Right away, they headed toward the *Titanic*'s last reported position.

MAKING THE MOST OF COMPETITION

Even though Bob had been stressed about someone else finding the *Titanic* before he had the chance to look, the information the other people provided from their trips turned out to be helpful. For example, one rich guy from Texas had paid for three unsuccessful expeditions to find the shipwreck. He reported that the high seas had damaged equipment, and he gave another helpful clue: the location of a propeller.

Bob formed a plan. He would have to be more patient than the people who had rushed out to sea before him. He would have to meticulously explore the area in a way they hadn't. He would have to ask better questions, like, "How had everyone missed a ship standing as tall as an 11-story building on the ocean floor?"

He realized that other explorers had used state-of-the-art sonar to scan for the ship, but maybe sonar wasn't the way to go. From his previous expeditions, he knew full well that the ocean was its own world with mountain ranges and rifts. If the *Titanic* had dropped into a canyon or behind a ridge, even something as long as six commercial airplanes might not show up. But *Argo* had cameras . . .

Soon, Bob's strategy was simply to *look* for the ship.

The crew turned to historic survivor eyewitness accounts that claimed the ship had snapped in half before sinking, along with logs from other ships that had been traveling in the area the night the *Titanic* went down. *If* the vessel had indeed split—because some of the witnesses had different stories, so it was tough to say—debris from the wreck could have drifted farther south than the area where people had searched. For days they scanned new areas with *Argo*'s cameras, hoping to find a telltale sign of scattered wreckage that might lead them to the ship.

This method only gave the team tons of scrolling footage of the seafloor and not a whole lot more.

BOB BALLARD (POINTING) AND TOM CROOK (SEATED IN MIDDLE) DURING THE SEARCH FOR THE *TITANIC*, 1986. (PHOTO COURTESY OF WOODS HOLE OCEANOGRAPHIC INSTITUTION ARCHIVES)

They had only four days left to complete their expedition, and the team was exhausted. They had been working around the clock with nothing to show for it. More importantly, they were running out of time. A sense of failure took over.

Suddenly, *Argo* picked up a glimmer on its camera at

1 o'clock in the morning. The crew perked up. Was that a metal plate?

Five minutes later, the robot caught the image of something that gave them all the hope they had almost lost—it was a boiler! The search team knew that the *Titanic* had been powered by 29 of these coal-fed boilers.

"Although we had read a great deal about the *Titanic* and studied many pictures, none of that research prepared us for the impact of the actual sightings," Bob recalled. "The race to find the *Titanic* was over. We had plumbed the eternal darkness with our tethered eyeball, and we had found the unmarked grave. For science, a new era in deep-sea exploration could finally begin."

ROV *JASON JUNIOR* PEERS INTO THE *TITANIC* WRECK THROUGH A HULL WINDOW. (PHOTO COURTESY OF WOODS HOLE OCEANOGRAPHIC INSTITUTION ARCHIVES)

Finding the sunken treasure had consumed hours' worth of camera time for the little robots. But now that they knew exact coordinates, it was time to give *Alvin* a shot and see the grave for themselves.

With success and fame surrounding him for the discovery, Bob was able to secure time with *Alvin* for a more in-depth expedition the following summer of 1986. *Alvin* would bring along its own tethered ROV named *Jason Junior* (*JJ*), which could work in tandem with the submersible to capture camera footage of places *Alvin* couldn't reach. Someone inside *Alvin* would then operate the ROV.

Bob descended on July 13 with Ralph Hollis as pilot and Dudley Foster as copilot. He noticed a change in the mucky seafloor. It sloped upward in an unnatural way, as though something had plowed the area to make it so steep. That's when they saw it for the first time.

"And there, in front of us, a black wall of steel plates rose up and up, seemingly forever," Bob remembered. "Riveted together in Belfast long before any of us were born, it stretched upward farther than we could see into the inky blackness. It was as if we had discovered the ancient walls of Troy in the middle of the night. The walls of *Titanic* stood before us, frozen in time."

They didn't have much time to explore the sunken treasure, unfortunately. Seawater was leaking into *Alvin*'s battery bank. The mission had to end, and they went to the surface.

TAKE TWO

The next dive, *JJ* experienced leaking, too. In an almost creepy way, both trips had some type of compartment flooding when approaching the ship that sank after its compartments had filled . . .

If they returned to the surface to fix *JJ*, they wouldn't have time to dive again that day, so *Alvin* ventured on without its ROV pal. The crew was frustrated, but they continued with the dive, approaching the *Titanic* head-on.

When *Alvin* approached the wreck, they forgot their irritation and stared in awe.

"All of a sudden, an enormous prow emerged from the darkness, not 30 feet away, as if still plowing ahead under full power—and on the brink of running us over," Bob continued. "Once again, we gawked in amazement."

THE BOW OF THE *TITANIC*. (IMAGE COURTESY OF NOAA AND THE RUSSIAN ACADEMY OF SCIENCES)

They swooped upward toward where the decks should have been. Marine organisms had devoured the wood over the years. Jagged metal from where the *Titanic* had snapped in two before sinking made the explorers worried the sharp points would pierce *Alvin*'s fiberglass sail and pin them underwater. Fortunately, they returned to the surface unharmed. Once aboard the research vessel, they had to repair *JJ*. On the third dive, Dudley piloted *Alvin* with Bob and Martin Bowen aboard. Once they landed, Martin took control of *JJ* and began exploring. They saw a crystal light fixture still dangling from its wire, doorknobs, unopened champagne bottles, bathtubs, shoes, and more. They even came across a safe with its back side rusted off.

ALVIN HONORS THE DEAD

But much unlike other adventures, where *Alvin* was tasked with collecting materials from the seafloor, Bob didn't want to remove anything from the *Titanic*. Instead, the team left behind a gravestone plaque on the stern to honor the men, women, and children who had died.

It read:

> *In memory of those souls who perished with the "Titanic" April 14/15, 1912.*
>
> *Dedicated to William H. Tantum, IV whose dream to find the "Titanic" has been realized by Dr. Robert D. Ballard.*
>
> *The officers and members of the Titanic Historical Society Inc. 1986.*

"Looking at *Titanic*'s shattered stern as we pulled away," Bob recalled, "I could think only of the passengers who had stayed on board, crowding closer and closer together on that deck as it tilted higher and higher—and then snapped off from the rest of the ship."

Dead Men Tell No Tales, but Their Ships Do

When we think of deep-sea explorers stumbling upon an old shipwreck from the days of pirates, we tend to imagine a ghost-like vessel with torn sails—fish swimming in and out of holes in the wood and precious jewels glittering from a treasure chest. In reality, after hundreds of years, there's simply no ship left, because—as we've learned from Ruth Turner—deep-sea creatures eat wood. But that doesn't mean there's nothing left to find . . .

In 2012, marine scientists from North Carolina State University,

Duke University, and the University of Oregon set out on an expedition led by Cindy Van Dover to search for a lost mooring that had been deployed off the coast of North Carolina. The autonomous underwater vehicle *Sentry* was on duty, scanning the seafloor, when suddenly, it picked up something shadowy.

The crew decided to take *Alvin* down for a look. There were red bricks, a long iron chain, glass bottles, pottery, a compass, and other navigational instruments.

The team realized they had discovered the remains of an 18th- or early 19th-century shipwreck.

Bring in the Archaeologists!

They called the Maritime Heritage Program of the National Oceanic and Atmospheric Administration (NOAA). Dr. James Delgado, director of the Maritime Heritage Program, said the area used to be a popular trade route, but it became known as the "graveyard of the Atlantic."

"The find is exciting, but not unexpected," he said. "Violent storms sent down large numbers of vessels off the Carolina coasts, but few have been located because of the difficulties of depth and

working in an offshore environment."

Cindy said the accidental find
illustrates the rewards and the
challenges of working in the deep
ocean. "We discovered a shipwreck
but, ironically, the lost mooring was
never found."

The quest for lost ships contin-
ues to captivate us, and the ones
that are discovered offer us information about the trade routes
and battles from the past. *Alvin*
hasn't always been involved in
their discovery, but its robot bud-
dies often are. Here's a glimpse at
some fun things ROVs have helped
us discover . . .

Finding the Bismarck

In 1989—just four years after finding the *Titanic*—Bob Ballard found the German battleship *Bismarck*, which sank in 1941 during World War II.

"This was very chilling because, when we first came across her with our remotely operated vehicle, *Argo*, you could still see swastikas painted on the bow and stern," Bob said, noting that this was actually surprising because the Nazis had painted over the swastikas when they left German waters. "And then when she was sunk only a few days later, the paint was so fresh that it sprawled away, revealing a second coat of paint of the swastikas."

The Black Sea Preserves Ancient Evidence

Bob said his favorite place to explore shipwrecks is in the Black Sea, which used to be a freshwater sea during the Ice Age. When it was flooded, the water came in and went stagnant, and as a result, the Black Sea is dead from 328 feet down. The Black Sea is the largest reservoir of dissolved hydrogen sulfide, which is a deadly gas that kills everything.

"As a result, shipwrecks in the Black Sea are absolutely in mint condition," he said, pointing out that amphoras (ancient clay jars) found in the Black Sea still show the beeswax used to seal the pottery or the impeccable remains of a human from 550 BCE.

"What I love to tell people is that the next generation of explorers that are in middle school right now will explore more of earth than all previous generations combined," Bob continued. "And they're the ones that are going to unlock these two million, three million years of human history that's preserved in the deep sea."

CHAPTER 10

Alvin's First Female Pilot

Alvin's adventures have led to some amazing discoveries, but, perhaps even more important, the little sub also offers inspiration to future generations of scientists. Take Cindy Van Dover. Born in 1954, she was just a kid when *Alvin* was first introduced to the world. She remembered first reading about the submersible when she was in elementary school, and a seed was planted.

"I thought, 'We're going to the moon. Wouldn't it be great to go to the bottom of the sea?'" she said. "I was entranced by oceanography."

That fascination set the wheels in motion. Between

her natural curiosity, growing up about 5 miles from the ocean, and her mom's habit of gathering plants and leaves to study, Cindy soon started her own collection. But her specimens were a bit more *wiggly*. She loved the creatures that lived in the tidepools.

STARBURST ANEMONE IN A TIDEPOOL. (PHOTO BY SARA HEINTZELMAN/NOAA)

"I thought the invertebrates were fascinating!" she said. "They were so different from me and my dog and my parakeet. I was curious how they made a living with all those weird appendages."

In high school, Cindy went to a shellfish research lab to study clams. She had to take care of the rats and cockroaches, too, which wasn't always fun, but she was right at home in a science lab.

In college, she became interested in how invertebrates timed their reproduction. Since oysters spawned in warmer temperatures, she wanted to know how creatures reproduced in the frigid waters of the deep sea.

TRY, TRY AGAIN

In the early 1980s, she found herself applying for the joint PhD program between MIT and WHOI. She didn't get accepted. She applied again. Again, she was declined. Finally, after the third attempt, she made it into the program.

One day, while studying hydrothermal vents, Cindy visited *Lulu, Alvin*'s support ship.

"I thought, man, it would be great to be a pilot," she said.

From there, she worked with Bob Ballard, a seasoned oceanographer. She would ask anyone who had an available berth—which is kind of like a spare bed—if she could go on cruises with them.

"Turns out, just asking is a great way to get opportunities," Cindy said.

While on one cruise in 1985, she told a crew member that she was interested in piloting *Alvin*. He suggested she help get the sub ready for a day of diving. She had to get up at 5 a.m., and they put her to work.

"Every day on that cruise, I got up and did things—hang weights, polish windows," she recalled.

In between chores, she checked the dive board, which is the list the chief scientist puts up to show who's diving inside *Alvin* the next day. Each time, her name wasn't there.

"Then one day, there was my name, so I knew I was going to dive the next day, and I could *not* sleep," she said. "The thing that sticks in my mind is standing at the railing, watching the sun set, and looking at the surface of the water, thinking, 'Tomorrow morning, I'm going to be all the way down . . . underneath a mile and a half of water.'"

The wonder she experienced from that very first dive only fed her desire to one day get in the pilot's seat. As a student of science, she knew that sometimes to get what you want, you have to write what's called a *proposal*. That proposal is basically a request for a grant (money) so you can achieve a certain goal. She sent one in to the National Science Foundation, asking for the money that would help her get trained and certified.

"But when the reviews came back, the reviewers were vicious, really vicious," Cindy said.

Even many years later, she remembered those grant reviewers saying they would never trust a scientist as a pilot. "They said things like, 'Why does *she* want to become a pilot?' It was awful. I was just in tears when I got those reviews. So that wasn't the way I was going to get funded."

ALVIN FACTS

THOSE who want the chance to work with *Alvin* have to go through a Pilot-in-Training (PIT) program. But before that, aspiring pilots typically start off as technicians, helping in any way possible and getting familiar with the vessel. *Alvin* has a lot of gadgets to get used to! This takes a couple months—and during that time, PIT trainees are trying to decide if they like working with *Alvin*, and the crew is trying to decide if the new person is a good fit, too.

After that, it's lots of training dives, learning everything about *Alvin*'s electrical systems, and taking tests. WHOI and the navy review board grill new applicants. The time this takes can vary from person to person, but the entire process can take about two to four years.

As it turned out, the navy decided it needed a maintenance manual for *Alvin* while the sub was in for an overhaul. There had never been one—the knowledge had all been passed on from one pilot to the next. But the navy wanted something with check-offs, and someone needed to write it.

Cindy jumped at the chance. She spent her mornings working on her dissertation to earn her PhD. In the afternoon, she'd head to the hangar where *Alvin* was undergoing an overhaul. The mechanics handed her pieces of paper with information on the parts and things she needed to know. Writing the manual helped her understand *Alvin* from the inside out. It also kept her close to the sub . . .

After working for free for almost a year, Cindy was finally hired as an apprentice electrician for *Alvin*. Shortly after she joined the team, the lead electrician left for another job, and she took over. She had to learn *everything*—and fast!

She went from knowing the difference between Phillips and flathead screwdrivers to understanding complex hydraulics systems. If you get stuck in *Alvin* at the bottom of the ocean, you have to know how to fix it. Seasoned pilot Dudley Foster suggested she sit inside *Alvin* with her eyes closed and learn where every switch is by heart. When the sub came up for cleaning, she did just that. This work led her to the opportunity of joining the pilot training program.

CINDY VAN DOVER, THE FIRST FEMALE *ALVIN* PILOT. (PHOTO BY ROD CATANACH © WOODS HOLE OCEANOGRAPHIC INSTITUTION)

A NEW GIG OPENS DOORS— OR HATCHES

All of that hard work and free labor paid off in the end. The day after Cindy earned her PhD, she joined the Alvin Group and became its first female certified pilot in 1990. Her debut mission was to bring Elana Leithold and Cynthia Hugget on a research expedition. It was the first-ever all-women dive!

Despite her training and experience, Cindy admitted that sometimes she had anxiety about piloting—but mostly when she was asleep. She'd have dreams that something terrible was happening under her watch.

In reality, she only recalled one time that truly rattled her . . .

She was on a mission near the Mid-Atlantic Ridge for a geology dive. The two researchers aboard noticed a fissure (or a crack in the seafloor). They wanted to go inside it and take a closer look, so Cindy wiggled *Alvin* into the crack. But then she remembered that there had been warnings about a series of microearthquakes in that exact area.

In fact, they had even talked about what they would do if there was an earthquake while they were diving in

114

Alvin. Scientists, of course, are naturally curious, and Cindy said the first response is often, "Well, we're going to go look at it!" She even got caught up in the moment, inching closer—until she snapped out of it.

"I thought, 'This is a really stupid place to be,'" she said. "I hyperventilated and said, 'We're getting out of here!'"

She immediately reversed the vessel and brought them all back safely.

Cindy served as an *Alvin* pilot for about two and a half years, noting that she absorbed a lot of great information from scientists in other fields during that time. She went on to lead research and teach courses at the University of Oregon, the University of Alaska, the College of William & Mary, and Duke University—where she served as the first female director of the marine laboratory in 2006. While her piloting days might have been over, she loved the adventures she was able to experience and the challenge of proving herself in a male-dominated industry.

"Looking back, I had built this thing in my mind of what I was trying to do—I had to do it," she recalled. "The thing that kept me from quitting, even when it was tough, was that I felt I would be letting down my gender."

From the moment she stood at the railing—watching the sunset and knowing she would dive in *Alvin* for the very first time the next morning—to the heartache and hard work, Cindy said she will never be the same.

"Diving in *Alvin*, it's spiritual," she said. "It changes the way you look at the world."

CRAZY CRITTERS

In 2005, scientists using *Alvin* stumbled upon a white crab with long "fur" on its legs and nicknamed it the yeti crab. Cindy admitted she didn't get too worked up when she first discovered the crab with Michel Segonzac. They saw lots of undersea creatures, and at the time, she waved off Michel's comment that there was "a weird crab over here."

But then he said, "Oh, there's another . . . and another!"

Finally, the pilot picked it up.

"I thought it was unusual, but I didn't get a eureka moment," Cindy said.

That's the nature of discovery and research, though. Oftentimes, you don't know you have something new until you bring it back to the lab to study it later.

But in the months that followed, her study of the yeti crab's shape—its morphology—made her realize that it was not just a new species. It belonged to an entirely new family of crab. It looks somewhat like a lobster, with its long body, but scientists decided it's more closely related to a hermit crab. They also began to study its weird hairs.

Caught on camera, the yeti crabs hold their hairy claws over the hydrothermal vents as mineral-rich fluid flows up from the seafloor. It's not entirely clear yet why they do this. But researchers think it might be to store bacteria, which can serve as a snack for later.

While the yeti crabs like the heat of the vents, the fate of that first crab wasn't so hot. It now sits in a sample jar at the French National History Museum in Paris.

CHAPTER 11

The Lost City

One cold winter night in 2000, geologist Gretchen Früh-Green sat in the *Atlantis*'s control room, watching live camera footage from the ROV *Argo* that was scanning the ocean depths below. Her team was imaging the cliffs of the Atlantic Massif, which is a large mountain range along the Mid-Atlantic Ridge. On a mission led by Donna Blackman, Gretchen joined fellow scientists Deborah Kelley and Jeffrey Karson and crew aboard the research cruise as they tried to understand exactly how this unusually tall mountain had formed and changed over 2 million years.

But watching video from the research vessel late in

the evening as *Argo* quietly towed along on its line below was sometimes a real snooze. You could sit by for hours without capturing too much.

Fortunately for Gretchen, that wasn't the case. Out of nowhere, at about 2,300 miles east of Florida and 2,600 feet beneath the surface, something massive came into view.

It was ghostly white. Then it disappeared.

CARBONATE SPIRES IN THE LOST CITY VENT FIELD. (PHOTO COURTESY OF IFE, URI-IAO, UW, LOST CITY SCIENCE PARTY; NOAA/OAR/OER; THE LOST CITY 2005 EXPEDITION)

As the camera moved, it showed another just like it. And another.

A DEEP-SEA JELLYFISH UNDULATING AT THE LOST CITY. (PHOTO COURTESY OF IFE, URI-IAO, UW, LOST CITY SCIENCE PARTY; NOAA/OAR/OER; THE LOST CITY 2005 EXPEDITION)

Gretchen ran to tell Deborah and Jeffrey that "something" had shown up on the camera. They decided to take a dip in *Alvin* to see it for themselves.

What they found there was shocking. Completely by accident while searching for different information, they had found a field of carbonate mineral "chimneys" towering about 200 feet above the seafloor. The structures rose from the ground in what looked like a city full of skyscrapers. They had found a hydrothermal vent field.

The explorers dubbed it "Lost City" in part because it sits on top of the mountain range named Atlantis (much like the boat the researchers were on). It also reminded them of Greek and Roman columns left behind from ancient times.

Pilot Bruce Strickrott remembered the moment these scientists discovered the area. "They were giddy!" he recalled. "You watch these senior scientists studying mantle rock discover something completely new and watch their careers change."

FROM LEFT: GRETCHEN FRÜH-GREEN (GEOLOGIST) AND ADELIE DELACOUR (RESEARCHER) IN LAB DURING THE LOST CITY CRUISE. (PHOTO BY JOHN HAYES © WOODS HOLE OCEANOGRAPHIC INSTITUTION)

HOW ARE LOST CITY VENTS DIFFERENT FROM BLACK SMOKERS?

While the Lost City chimneys are a type of hydrothermal vent, they're created in a different way than the ones that are referred to as "black smokers." Instead of billowing black clouds emerging along a volcanic mountain range, the tall white chimneys discharge gas-rich fluids that look more like heat waves rippling over the asphalt on a hot summer day.

Hydrothermal fluid venting at the site is about 200 degrees Fahrenheit, which isn't nearly as hot as the black smokers that get up to 760 degrees Fahrenheit. Black smokers are formed when seawater circulates through and reacts with hot volcanic rocks. The resulting hot, buoyant fluid discharges at the seafloor and turns black as the sulfide minerals precipitate out to form chimneys. But at Lost City, seawater reacts with rocks from Earth's mantle in a process called *serpentinization*. This type of reaction produces hydrogen- and methane-rich fluids, along with the chimneys made of carbonate minerals.

The explorers gathered a sample of the chimney material to study and soon made another discovery. Even though the towers had seemed lifeless to the naked eye, under the microscope, researchers found itty-bitty creatures called *microorganisms*!

Lost City, they realized, is home to an exceptional type of hydrothermal vent, in that it produces acetate, formate, hydrogen, and alkaline fluids, which are all substances that may have been key to the first emergence of life on our planet. So while the vents found in 1977 challenged scientists' thinking on how and where life could exist, this vent field offered a clue about where it possibly all started.

"It is one more bit of evidence about where life may have originated," Deborah explained.

CRAZY CRITTERS

TURNS out, it's not so tough to find an octopus—not if you're cruising over an octopus garden inside *Alvin*, of course.

Two miles below the surface in the Monterey Bay National Marine Sanctuary, thousands of mother octopuses brood their eggs. The 2018 discovery of this place was yet another fortunate accident.

Scientists were exploring the Davidson Seamount—an

underwater oasis about 80 miles off the coast of Monterey, California. They were using *Alvin* to research sponges and corals to see how far their habitat ranged, when they came across the octopuses, now given the scientific name of *Muusoctopus robustus*.

A GROUPING OF *MUUSOCTOPUS* POSITIONED IN A BROODING POSTURE, PROTECTING THEIR EGGS. (PHOTO COURTESY OF OET/NOAA)

Chad King of the National Oceanic and Atmospheric Administration (NOAA) explained that the mothers were there because of the warm water, which is unusual because most octopuses thrive in cold water.

This particular species of octopus is especially unique. It folds its mantle (or head) and tentacles over its eggs, so that its mouth is exposed. And it takes at least *two years* to hatch its eggs. (That's a long time to wait for a baby to be born!)

Even though we've now learned that the octopuses stay near Monterey for a long time, Chad wants to know, "Do they all come at once and leave at once?"

He proposed there is a revolving door of mothers coming and going at different times. The important thing to note, he said, was that by protecting the corals and sponges in this designated sanctuary, they're now protecting this nursery of octopus mothers.

"It's another reason why we need to protect more of the world's oceans."

CHAPTER 12

Teacher Takes a Dive

While *Alvin*'s adventures pushed science forward, for Carolyn Sheild—a former teacher at Clarke Middle School in Lexington, Massachusetts—science pushed her to *Alvin*. Carolyn taught science for years, but the largest lesson she aimed to give her students was to follow their dreams. After all, reaching for the stars is exactly how she landed the chance to plunge into the ocean . . .

It all started in 2000, when her mentor, marine geochemist Susan Humphris, asked for a favor. Susan was on a mission—to give kids a hands-on approach to science. Susan and Dan Fornari—WHOI senior scientist of geology and geophysics—had created a neat website called Dive and Discover. It was an interactive platform that allowed kids to communicate with scientists and receive updates on research. But the site was new, and Susan needed some outside opinions—and who better to test it than the students it was meant for?

Remember Susan? She was the one who first took a dive in *Alvin* in 1986 when the biggest-yet-discovered hydrothermal vent site in the Atlantic was found!

Susan urged students to not be put off by tough topics.

"You have to have a love of exploring and discovering, but you also have to back that love of exploring and discovering with a foundation in the sciences and mathematics," she said. "That allows you to take that science and apply it to the ocean. In order to understand what you're exploring and discovering, you've also got to be able to explain it."

Since Susan had inspired Carolyn while she earned her teaching credentials and completed her master's degree in sea star predation and sponges, the women already knew each other. And Susan asked if Carolyn's class would be willing to be the guinea pigs. Carolyn's students helped by pointing out any issues with the website. At the same time, they would follow the scientists' daily updates, and students could send emails and get their questions answered while the scientists were at sea.

It was fun for the kids, but it also inspired Carolyn.

"That website was my porthole into really taking off with more ocean science in my classroom," she said.

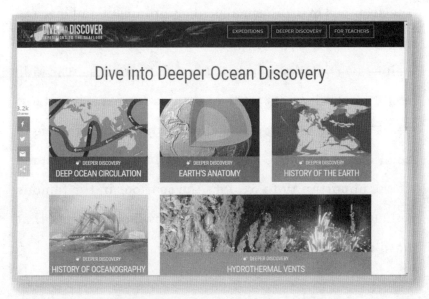

SCREENSHOT OF THE DIVE AND DISCOVER WEBSITE, TAKEN ON MARCH 12, 2023.

Later in 2002, Susan invited Carolyn to a three-day workshop for the NSF-funded Ridge2000 program, which brought together about 25 teachers from all over the country to discuss ways to bring deep-ocean science into the classroom.

Carolyn then got her class involved in the Student Experiments at Sea (SEAS) program, which was made for middle and high school students "who want to learn science by doing science." The students were able to study the deep-sea hydrothermal vent environment and learn to ask questions like real researchers. Ridge2000 scientists helped by contributing their time and expertise. The kids could give scientists their questions for experiments at sea. The class that performed well could win a chance to send their teacher to sea inside *Alvin*. Carolyn dreamed of the opportunity to explore the seafloor in the famous submersible! And she wanted to show her students that hard work could achieve great things.

She met with the kids before and after school to create a proposal with all the steps for the scientific method.

"There was a lot of figuring things out," she said. "The kids did the research and figured out the best questions to ask."

They tested a crab's reaction to sound in an experiment called "Do You Hear What I Hear?" The experiment involved *Alvin* taking pictures of crabs while it was emitting sounds. They watched the behaviors of the crabs— some scuttled away, some stayed. The kids made graphs of the experiment and wrote a final report.

While they won best proposal, they didn't win in the category to send Carolyn to sea.

Finally, in 2005, Carolyn's class submitted a proposal, and scientists performed an experiment, called "Crabs Catch of the Day," which investigated feeding preferences of crabs. They won best report overall for designing and analyzing the experiment, and in 2007, Carolyn went aboard *Alvin*'s research vessel for an entire month. She was told ahead of time that diving inside *Alvin* wasn't a guarantee, since the scientists funded for the dive program have priority.

On this very trip, *Alvin* made the world's longest-distance call—the first-ever phone conversation between someone in space and someone at the bottom of the ocean. NASA astronaut Sunita Williams was orbiting in the

AN EXTREME-LONG-DISTANCE CALL FROM THE DEPTHS OF THE OCEAN TO THE REACHES OF SPACE. (PHOTO OF INTERNATIONAL SPACE STATION, TOP, NASA; PHOTO OF *ALVIN*, BOTTOM, EXPEDITION TO THE DEEP SLOPE/NOAA/OER)

International Space Station while chatting with biologist Tim Shank on the seafloor.

Carolyn had to wait for three weeks before Tim asked if she'd like a turn to dive.

Like a turn? Are you kidding? She was thrilled to accept! The night before, she went to the deck a little afraid. But she

CAROLYN SHEILD CLIMBING INTO *ALVIN*. (PHOTO COURTESY OF CAROLYN SHEILD)

looked at *Alvin* and pushed aside any doubts. Her dream was finally coming true.

Filled with excitement, Carolyn rose early the next morning and plunged down, down, down into the watery depths. Underwater, she saw two lantern fish facing each other. She spoke into her recorder and explained what the world beneath the surface was like. Tim encouraged her to take a moment to "realize where you are. Just be there."

ALVIN FACTS

BEFORE a new person plunges into the deep with *Alvin*, there's a required "safety check." The crew members introduce new divers to features inside the sub and basic emergency procedures. By the time the lesson is over, about 40 minutes have passed.

But the main reason for the check is to see if a newbie will freak out in the small space. While inside, the pros watch for signs that someone might be experiencing claustrophobia.

Geochemist Susan Humphris can attest to the close quarters.

"When you've got three of you in a six-foot-diameter sphere, just the act of putting on a sweater requires everybody's cooperation," she joked.

Even those who pass the test still might not get the full 8 to 10 hours. During a dive, the pilot checks the systems every 30 minutes. If there's any electrical system problem, the mission is aborted, and the crew heads home early. Safety first!

Carolyn saw hardened lava and smokers, and she also had the task of searching for experiment equipment that previously had been left behind.

CALLING HOME FROM UNDER THE SEA

While in the sub, Carolyn got to make her own long-distance call to Clarke Middle School.

"They said over the PA system, 'The announcements are special this afternoon—we have Carolyn Sheild speaking to us from the bottom of the ocean!'" she remembered.

Thanks to this experience, Carolyn always told her students to follow their passion.

"My heart was just so glad and so grateful that I had that opportunity."

CHAPTER 13

Striking Oil, but Not Striking It Rich

Sadly, *Alvin*'s missions aren't always glitzy treasure-finding adventures or making dreams come true. Sometimes, the sub is tasked with the grim chore of investigating the human impact on our planet when things go wrong—and things definitely went wrong one April night in 2010 . . .

An oil rig floating in the Gulf of Mexico was going through its regular operations, which included pulling oil from wells that had been drilled into the seabed. The BP Deepwater Horizon offshore company rig—a type of oil-drilling platform built for the ocean—was positioned in the water off the coast of Louisiana in a valley of the continental shelf. Once it was done funneling oil from about 18,000 feet below the seafloor through a riser (a tube to pull oil from underground to the ship above), it was supposed to seal off the well for later use.

Suddenly, a surge of natural gas blasted through the well's concrete core. That gas traveled up the rig's riser to the platform. Faster than anyone could respond, the gas ignited and killed 11 workers—Jason Anderson, Aaron Dale Burkeen, Donald Clark, Stephen Curtis, Gordon Jones, Roy Wyatt Kemp, Karl Dale Kleppinger Jr., Blair Manuel, Dewey Revette, Shane Roshto, and Adam Weise.

The rig began to sink, tearing apart the riser. Oil flowed into the water of the Gulf.

Underwater cameras later showed a cloud of black oil churning out thousands of barrels of oil per day. People worked frantically to try to stop the contamination.

For months, oil pumped from the broken wellhead before engineers were able to seal it off in July. Anywhere from 134 million to 206 million gallons of oil had poured into the Gulf of Mexico, spreading across 1,300 miles and causing massive harm and death to wildlife

FIREBOAT RESPONSE CREWS BATTLE THE BLAZING REMNANTS OF THE OFFSHORE OIL RIG DEEPWATER HORIZON. (PHOTO COURTESY OF US COAST GUARD)

and ecosystems. A lot of the oil floated to the surface, and cleanup experts even set fire to it—trying to get rid of the oil in a procedure called a *controlled burn*.

A CONTROLLED BURN OF OIL FROM THE BP DEEPWATER HORIZON OIL SPILL SENDS TOWERS OF FIRE HUNDREDS OF FEET INTO THE AIR OVER THE GULF OF MEXICO. (PHOTO BY PETTY OFFICER FIRST CLASS JOHN MASSON, US COAST GUARD)

But some of that crude oil attached to particles in the water and sank to the seafloor. And in December of that year, *Alvin* received a new mission. This one involved showing the world just how much had been damaged.

Thanks to funding from the National Science Foundation's Rapid Response Program, *Alvin*—paired with WHOI's autonomous underwater vehicle named *Sentry*—was able to help researchers study the impact the oil had on coral communities.

Like the *Argo/Jason* system that was developed beforehand to explore shipwrecks, *Sentry* was another tool to explore the water, but this little robot wasn't tethered to the ship. It could swim freely and dive to depths of nearly 20,000 feet, while capturing photos and using a high-tech sensor system to scan the seafloor.

What they discovered was shocking. Explorers combing the area realized that—in a matter of months following the April spill—all the corals were either dead, dying, or completely gone. The brown gunk was everywhere. The effort to clean up the mess was no match for the man-made disaster. Despite controlled burns on the surface and the expanse of the ocean's waters, this was evidence that the oil may have spread around but wouldn't simply *disappear*.

A COMPARISON OF NORMAL CORAL WITH SOME DEAD SKELETAL MATERIAL COVERED BY TYPICAL SECONDARY COLONIZATION (LEFT) AND A WILTING, DYING CORAL COVERED WITH OIL PLUME DEBRIS (RIGHT). (PHOTOS COURTESY OF LOPHELIA II 2010, NOAA OER AND BOEM)

Through ongoing research, they learned the spill had a long-term impact. By 2021, it was discovered that a food source many large marine mammals eat—a group called *lantern fishes*—had shrunk by over 80 percent since 2011. Krill, which whales love to eat, had been reduced by over 90 percent.

THE SILVER LINING

But thanks to *Alvin*'s work and the ongoing research over the years, scientists have also discovered some pretty neat things . . .

While searching, they discovered that the Gulf had more animal diversity than they realized. Researchers also discovered that some animals—like sparrows that were eating oil-coated crustaceans—had a natural defense built into their genetic makeup that made them immune to the pollutants. This gave them a clue about how some species had survived in their environments, even after they'd been polluted. So even though our studies and efforts to rebuild the Gulf will remain a point of focus for many going into the future, these types of discoveries have given scientists new tools and information that will help them better understand and protect the environment.

CHAPTER 14

What's Next?

As the world's longest-operating deep-sea submersible, *Alvin* has been through a lot. But its
ongoing overhauls keep it in tip-top shape to meet our
world's evolving need for information.

Following the redesign of the personal sphere in
2005, a more extensive, two-phase overhaul began in
2011, so the sub could be reconstructed to keep pace with
technology and last for years to come. Even though she's
not an engineer, WHOI scientist Susan Humphris was a
principal investigator for the *Alvin* upgrade. Her job was
to keep the project on budget and on time, while meeting scientific requirements defined by the community.

ALVIN FACTS

ABOUT every three years, *Alvin* goes through a major overhaul. Mechanical engineers take it completely apart, upgrade and repair its pieces, then put it all back together again. During that time, they also check safety systems. Since this happens so frequently, none of the original *Alvin* remains.

The now-retired pilot and mechanic Dudley Foster had a hand in *Alvin*'s overhauls. He also checked on the sub before, during, and after every dive.

When Dudley first joined the team in 1972, *Alvin* was rated for 6,000 feet, he said.

"It had an aluminum frame and a stainless-steel personnel sphere," he continued. "It got upgraded to a titanium sphere, which went to 12,000 feet."

The upgrade to titanium in the 1970s not only helped *Alvin* dive deeper, but it eliminated corrosion, which Dudley said used to be a big problem. He also watched the new ballast pump get installed. This system improved *Alvin*'s means for going up and down.

During the first upgrade phase, completed in 2013, *Alvin* was equipped with a new and larger sphere to provide more comfort for those inside.

The sub went from three to five viewports to improve visibility for the science observers and pilot. The upgrade also included new lighting, high-definition imaging systems, foam (for buoyancy), and an improved command and control system.

On adding new viewports, Susan said, "The earlier design for *Alvin* was purely for observation, and there was no overlap in the fields of view out of each of the viewports, but when they realized they could use the machine for sampling, they also realized you might want to see what the pilot was doing."

The team completed verification trials in 2014, which involved a series of tests to show that the upgrade was successful and safe for humans.

The second stage began in 2020, when *Alvin* returned to Woods Hole for a revamp in the midst of a global pandemic. This phase included an upgrade to bring the sub into deeper water—over 21,000 feet. This was up from about 15,000 feet before the upgrade was complete. At depths of 15,000 feet, researchers in *Alvin* had access to about 67 percent of the ocean floor. But now with an upgrade to 21,000 feet, 98 to 99 percent of the ocean floor can be explored.

The second phase also gave *Alvin* new higher horsepower thrusters and pressure housings, along with a beefed-up mechanical arm, which will help *Alvin* collect more samples.

Alvin finished its overhaul in the summer of 2021, ready for test dives to make sure it was able to dive more than 21,000 feet and explore even more places in the ocean. *Alvin* then had to go through a series of these tests to gain navy certification.

In August 2022, following the completion of its upgrades, *Alvin* successfully achieved science verification.

"We set a high bar for *Alvin*, and it easily met or exceeded expectations," said Anna Michel, WHOI's chief scientist for deep submergence. "*Alvin* is ready for science."

A MECHANICAL PERSPECTIVE

Danik Forsman is a mechanical section leader for the Alvin Group. He pilots the vessel every third dive day when at sea and goes to sea with *Alvin* about five months of the year to oversee its mechanical maintenance.

Danik was also part of the overhaul effort. Overseeing the mechanical teardown, he and his team exposed *Alvin*'s frame to inspect the sphere.

"This overhaul has a lot of mechanical work. There are some electrical upgrades, too, but all of the major mechanical systems are getting completely replaced," Danik said in January 2021. "We're going to have a brand-new hydraulics system, variable ballast, main ballast, trim. At the moment, my job has been testing the new variable ballast pump. I'm working on that for the new pump with the lead mechanical engineer, Fran Elder. We work hand in hand on all of these projects."

As lead mechanical engineer, Francis Elder said he was responsible for upgrading the submersible's weight and balance, its new frame and syntactic foam, changing the ballast systems, and adding new thrusters, a hydraulics system, and more.

"There are a lot of systems being upgraded, but the highlight of this whole upgrade for me is the variable ballast system," Francis said before they finished the upgrade. "That definitely has the most tentacles.

"The ballast system impacts how *Alvin* floats. A series of titanium spheres hold water and air to help the sub achieve neutral buoyancy when underwater.

"When we go to depth, we drop some of the weights that brought *Alvin* down," Francis continued. "We want to be neutral so we don't have to use our thrusters to maintain position vertically in the water. So we pump water in or out of the system to achieve neutral buoyancy. *Alvin* is a battery-powered vehicle, so we want to be as efficient as possible."

Even though *Alvin* has been around for a while, Francis

said that it's constantly receiving new technology. "It's been 50 years of tweaking, and that's what makes the sub so reliable."

ALVIN LOOKS TO THE FUTURE

With another round of upgrades and the new ability to dive to 21,000 feet, *Alvin* will continue to be an important tool for discovery. "There are environments that we're going to be able to go to that we didn't have access to in the past," said Adam Soule, Ocean Exploration Cooperative Initiative director and former WHOI scientist. "For example, there's a new type of volcanism that's been discovered in the oceans called Petit-spots."

WHOI biologist Tim Shank explained that these are places in the deep ocean where an oceanic plate dives underneath another one.

"There are these little structures that pop up that look like small seamounts," Tim said. "They're almost completely unexplored, but now *Alvin*'s going to open up this new door for us to be able to get to these places."

147

He went on to note that climate change is having a big impact, and our oceans, in turn, are changing as well.

"There are so many questions we have and so many issues that we have," Tim said. "*Alvin* is going to be a primary tool to meet those challenges."

But he marveled at the unity the little submersible had created in its 57 years.

SCIENTISTS CROWD AROUND THE BIO-BOXES AT THE FRONT OF *ALVIN*, EAGER TO SEE WHAT WAS COLLECTED ON THAT DAY'S DIVE. (PHOTO TAKEN IN THE GULF OF ALASKA, 2004, COURTESY OF NOAA OFFICE OF OCEAN EXPLORATION)

"*Alvin* has brought together geologists, geochemists, microbiologists, macrofaunal biologists, virologists—so many 'ologists' have come together because of *Alvin*, wanting to use *Alvin* together, understanding the system," Tim said. "This is astounding [that] this vehicle has done this over time for us and developed relationships and collaborations that led to even greater discoveries. And so, I always give *Alvin* credit for not just discovering vents but taking the human ideas of science and bringing them together with other people and pushing science forward, really accelerating the pace of discovery."

CONCLUSION

In its lifetime, *Alvin* has helped change minds, science, and lives.

The exploration and thrill of discovery left scientist Susan Humphris with an understanding of how important it is to work with scientists of all backgrounds—and to learn from one another.

"If you think about it as explaining natural things that you might see in the world and trying to understand how the world works—if you can maintain that fascination—you should be able to explore and pursue this field if that's what you want to do," she said. "We know less than 10 percent of our seafloor. That's a huge chunk of missing information left to uncover."

Pilot Bruce Strickrott can't express enough the way

Alvin has changed him and those he shuttles down to the seafloor. The thrill of finding something new never wears off.

"The best part was knowing you'd stumbled upon something that no one had seen and watching the reactions of the scientists . . . and the power of discovery on people's emotions," Bruce said.

He went on to say that everyone is a scientist. From the time we're little, we're fascinated with the world. We go outside and dig in the dirt, roll over rocks, and pick up leaves.

"That curiosity is built in," he added.

And for Cindy Van Dover, a scientist and *Alvin*'s first female pilot, the little submersible taught her something that gave her a great sense of power—something she wished she'd known as a kid.

"For me, it was about not being afraid to ask if I could do something like, 'Can I go on this cruise?'" Cindy said. "I could have just as easily thought they'd say no. You can't catch fish if you don't go fishing. You have to have your bait and your line, but you really can't catch fish until you put that line in the water. That's what asking

151

is. Get your gear, your kit—your experience—together and see what you can make of it. And don't be afraid."

As someone still involved with the *Alvin* program, Bruce wanted people to know that *Alvin* is not just some relic sitting in a museum. He hopes to see the vessel alive and well for at least another 50 years.

From watching how *Alvin* has critically changed the lives of those who have climbed aboard, Bruce has reaped the benefits of pursuing his own passion for being a pilot.

"Some people pursue the dollar, and they end up miserable," he said. "Chase your dreams, and what you'll find is you'll end up in a place you never expected."

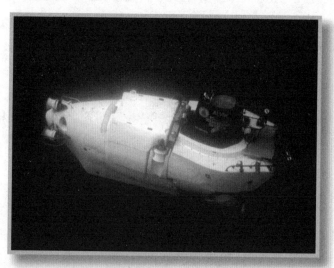

DSV *ALVIN*, PERHAPS THE MOST ACTIVE AND SUCCESSFUL RESEARCH SUB-MERSIBLE. (PHOTO BY R. CATANACH, OAR/NATIONAL UNDERSEA RESEARCH PROGRAM [NURP]; WOODS HOLE OCEANOGRAPHIC INSTITUTION)

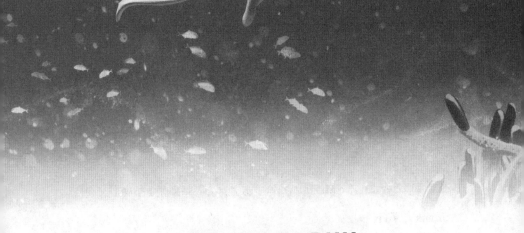

BIBLIOGRAPHY

RECORDED ARCHIVES

Froehlich, Harold. Interview with Frank Taylor. Woods Hole Oceanographic Institute oral history archives. 2003, 2004.

McCamis, Marvin. Interview with Frank Taylor. Woods Hole Oceanographic Institute oral history archives. 2003, 2004.

Vine, Allyn Collins. Interview with Dr. Gary Weir. Woods Hole
Oceanographic Institute oral history archives. 1989.

RECORDED INTERVIEWS WITH AUTHOR

Humphris, Susan
Sheild, Carolyn

Strickrott, Bruce

Van Dover, Cindy

BOOKS

Ballard, Robert D. *The Eternal Darkness* (Princeton, NJ: Princeton

University Press, 2000)

NEWS ARTICLES/PRESS RELEASES

Borunda, Alejandra, "We Still Don't Know the Full Impacts of the BP Oil

Spill, 10 Years Later," *National Geographic*, April 20, 2020, national

-geographic.com/science/article/bp-oil-spill-still-dont-know-effects

-decade-later?loggedin=true

Conniff, Richard, "When Continental Drift Was Considered Pseudo-

science," *National Geographic*, June 2012, smithsonianmag.com/science

-nature/when-continental-drift-was-considered-pseudoscience

-90353214/

Dicke, William, "Allyn Vine, 79, Dies; Proponent of Submersibles," *New

York Times*, Jan. 8, 1994, nytimes.com/1994/01/08/obituaries/allyn

-vine-79-dies-proponent-of-submersibles.html

Handwerk, Brian, "Titanic Is Falling Apart," *National Geographic,* Aug. 20, 2010, nationalgeographic.com/adventure/article/100818 -titanic-3-d-expedition-shipwreck-science-collapsing

Hines, Sandra, "Lost City Pumps Life-Essential Chemicals at Rates Unseen at Typical Black Smokers," Woods Hole Oceanographic Institution, Jan. 31, 2008, whoi.edu/oceanus/feature/lost-city -pumps-life-essential-chemicals-at-rates-unseen-at-typical-black -smokers/

Lucas, Tim, "Centuries-Old Shipwreck Discovered off NC Coast," *Duke Today*, July 17, 2015, today.duke.edu/2015/07/shipwreck

Madin, Kate, "Trailblazer in the Ocean," *Oceanus*, June 3, 2014, whoi.edu /oceanus/feature/trailblazer-in-the-ocean-depths/

Pallardy, Richard, "Deepwater Horizon Oil Spill," *Britannica*, Aug. 23, 2022, britannica.com/event/Deepwater-Horizon-oil-spill

Paris, Max, "Gulf deepwater coral shows damage after BP spill," CBC News, March 26, 2012, cbc.ca/news/science/gulf-deepwater-coral -shows-damage-after-bp-spill-1.1196002

Patowary, Kaushik, "The Sponge Divers of Greece," *Amusing Planet*, Nov. 28, 2016, amusingplanet.com/2016/11/the-sponge-divers-of -greece.html

Piecuch, Hannah, "Meet the *Alvin* 6500 Team: Danik Forsman," Woods Hole Oceanographic Institution, Jan. 21, 2021, whoi.edu/news -insights/content/alvin6500forsman

Rimler, Rose, "Revolutionary War-era Shipwreck discovered off North Carolina," *News Observer*, account.newsobserver.com/paywall /subscriber-only?resume=27514879&intcid=ab_archive

Roach, John, "*Titanic* Was Found During Secret Cold War Navy Mission," *National Geographic*, Nov. 21, 2017, nationalgeographic.com /history/article/titanic-nuclear-submarine-scorpion-thresher-ballard

Sullivan, Kathryn, "The Women of FAMOUS," *Oceanus*, March 1, 1998, whoi.edu/oceanus/feature/the-women-of-famous/

Thompson, Scott, "Centuries-Old Shipwreck Discovered Off North Carolina Coast," NC State College of Sciences, July 17, 2015, sciences.ncsu.edu /news/centuries-old-shipwreck-discovered-off-north-carolina-coast/

Whelan, Jean, "When Seafloor Meets Ocean, the Chemistry Is Amazing," Woods Hole Oceanographic Institution, Feb. 13, 2004, whoi.edu/oceanus /feature/when-seafloor-meets-ocean-the-chemistry-is-amazing/

WHOI press release: "Human-occupied vehicle *Alvin* successfully completes science verification," Woods Hole Oceanographic Institution, Aug. 23, 2022, whoi.edu/press-room/news-release/alvin -completes-science-verification/

Woodward, Aylin, "The *Titanic* Is Slowly but Surely Disappearing—Here's What the Wreck Looks Like Now," *Business Insider*, Oct. 6, 2019

ONLINE GOVERNMENT DOCUMENTS/ARCHIVES

"Atlantic 3800-Meter Radioactive Waste Disposal Site Survey: Sedimentary, Micromorphologic and Geophysical Analysis, 1978," United States Environmental Protection Agency, bit.ly/3EY4T80

"Deep Water: The Gulf Oil Disaster and the Future of Offshore Drilling," National Commission on the BP Deepwater Horizon Oil Spill and Offshore Drilling report to the president, 2011, govinfo.gov /content/pkg/GPO-OILCOMMISSION/pdf/GPO-OILCOMMISSION.pdf

"Fact Sheet on Ocean Dumping of Radioactive Waste Materials,"
United States Environmental Protection Agency, bit.ly/3eOgQCk

WEBSITES

"*Alvin* Submarine Discovers More Octopuses at 'Octopus Garden,'"
Sanctuary Integrated Monitoring Network, May 2, 2019, sanctuary
-simon.org/2019/05/alvin-submarine-discovers-more-octopuses-at
-octopus-garden/

"*Alvin*-US Navy," Bluebird Marine Systems Limited, bit.ly/3CJaNqS

"Antikythera Shipwreck," Woods Hole Oceanographic Institution,
whoi.edu/know-your-ocean/ocean-topics/ocean-human-lives
/underwater-archaeology/antikythera-shipwreck/

"Continental Drift Versus Plate Tectonics," *National Geographic*,
education.nationalgeographic.org/resource/continental-drift
-versus-plate-tectonics

"Current Biology: Chemosynthetic symbioses," Science Direct,
sciencedirect.com/science/article/pii/S0960982220310757

"The Evolution of *Alvin*," *National Geographic*, nationalgeograph⁚c
.com/news-features/evolution-of-alvin/

"Gulf of Mexico Oil Spill's Effects on Deep-Water Corals," National
Science Foundation, March 26, 2012, nsf.gov/news/news_summ.jsp
?cntn_id=123555

"H Bomb Lost in Spain," History.com, last updated Jan. 14, 2020.
history.com/this-day-in-history/h-bomb-lost-in-spain

"Historical Snapshot," Boeing, boeing.com/history/products/b-52
-stratofortress.page

"How the US Lost 4 Nukes," War History Online, Oct. 18, 2018. war-
historyonline.com/instant-articles/how-the-us-lost-4-nukes.html
?chrome=1

"Life *is* Full of Surprises," National Oceanic and Atmospheric Administration, last updated Dec. 18, 2017, oceanexplorer.noaa.gov
/explorations/05lostcity/background/overview/overview.html

"Maurice 'Doc' Ewing, biography (1906–1974)," Columbia Climate

School, ldeo.columbia.edu/the-vetlesen-prize/past-recipients
/maurice-doc-ewing

"Milestone-Proposal: *Alvin*: Deep-Sea Research Submersible,
1964–1965," IEEE Milestones Wiki, last updated Aug. 13, 2021,
ieeemilestones.ethw.org/Milestone-Proposal:ALVIN:_Deep-Sea
_Research_Submersible,_1964–1965

"Ocean Dumping," National Oceanic and Atmospheric Administration, last updated April 7, 2014, bit.ly/3satPkT

"Plate Tectonics," *National Geographic*, education
.nationalgeographic.org/resource/plate-tectonics

"Research reveals deep-ocean impact of the Deepwater Horizon oil
spill," PennState research, March 26, 2012, psu.edu/news/research
/story/research-reveals-deep-ocean-impact-deepwater-horizon-oil
-spill/

"Ruth Turner: Scientist, Underwater Pioneer," Science Network,
sciencenetwork.com/turner/rdt-bio.html

"Seafloor Magnetics," Dive and Discover, divediscover.whoi.edu/hot

-topics/magnetics/

"The 'Smoking' Gun," Woods Hole Oceanographic Institution,

whoi.edu/feature/history-hydrothermal-vents/discovery

/1979-2.html

"A Titanic Tale," *Oceanus*, Sept. 2, 2010, whoi.edu/oceanus/feature/a

-titanic-tale/

"What Are the Layers of the Earth?" *World Atlas*, worldatlas.com

/articles/the-layers-of-the-earth.html

"What is a bivalve mollusk?" National Ocean Service, last updated

Feb. 26, 2021, bit.ly/3TAOYAv

"What is a hydrothermal vent?" National Ocean Service, last updated

March 10, 2022, bit.ly/3eOcRG4

"What is a hydrothermal vent?" National Ocean Service, last updated

March 10, 2022, oceanservice.noaa.gov/facts/vents.html

"Women of the Museum of Comparative Zoology (MCZ)," Harvard
Library, last updated Oct. 20, 2022, guides.library.harvard.edu/fas
/WomenInBio/Turner

"Woods Hole Oceanographic Institution: A Guide to the Allyn Collins Vine Papers, 1937–1998," Woods Hole Oceanographic Institution, dlaweb.whoi.edu/PHP/FAID/faids_files/MC-01_Vine.html

"Woods Hole Oceanographic Institution: A Guide to the Papers of
Holger W. Jannasch, 1945–1998," Woods Hole Oceanographic Insti-
tution, dlaweb.whoi.edu/PHP/FAID_backup/faids_files/MC-41brief
_Jannasch.html

VIDEOS

"Diving to Octopus Garden in a Submarine," YouTube, uploaded by
Woods Hole Oceanographic Institution, Oct. 7, 2019, youtube.com
/watch?v=g7D5KNcBNaE

"Ocean Encounters: The Science of Shipwrecks," YouTube, uploaded
by Woods Hole Oceanographic Institution, May 6, 2020, youtube
.com/watch?v=R44tKAPpKOM

"'On the Surface' Part I," YouTube, uploaded by Shiftingbaselines,
Feb. 24, 2011, youtube.com/watch?v=bx62nYh8BTg

"Project Famous Mid-Ocean Undersea Study *Alvin* Submersible 51954."
YouTube, uploaded by PeriscopeFilm, Feb. 14, 2017, youtube.com
/watch?v=Rf0ykVISWfE

"Robert Ballard: Exploring the Ocean's Hidden Worlds." Youtube,
uploaded by TED, May 21, 2008, youtube.com/watch?v=qHU8G6icwsY

ACKNOWLEDGMENTS

I could fill this book with the names of people in my life worth thanking. The journey to becoming a published author started decades ago—I'd argue it started when I was a kid—and I honor those on my path who helped shape who I am now.

But since I must be brief, dear reader, I'll give you the upshot:

A very special thank-you to my agent, Moe Ferrara, who edited *way* too many of my manuscripts that never took off before we finally signed with Feiwel and Friends. I can't tell you how much it means to me that you continued to believe in my work.

To my rock-star editor, Holly West: Your expertise completely transformed this book. Thank you for your wordy wisdom, patience, and guidance throughout this process. I am truly grateful for the experience and excited for the road ahead.

Where would we be without a stellar editorial team? In ABC order, another huge thank-you to Julia Bianchi (designer), Jesse Cole (intern and fresh eyes reader), Bonnie Cutler (copyeditor), Brittany Groves (assistant editor and fresh eyes reader), Lelia Mander (production editor), and Kim Waymer (production manager). You all helped create a beautiful book about *Alvin*!

My sincere gratitude goes out to the amazing people who spent time to share with me their real-life experience with the submersible: Susan Humphris, Cindy Van Dover, Bruce Strickrott, and Carolyn Sheild. And thank you, Carolyn and Susan, for helping to review the material! Your guidance was invaluable, and I truly appreciate your additional time investment.

Of course, to my family for always loving and supporting me: my husband, Roger; kids, Nico, Carter, and McKayla; parents, Jackie and Sam Retelas, Peter and Pam Conner, and Dan and Sally Brown; siblings (every last one of you!); nephews, Evan Kramer and Dylan

Kenny; niece, Cassidy Morrison; and grandparents, who taught me that reading books together is one of the best ways to show love. I miss you every day, Sue and Nick Reckas.

Last but not least, to my friends, who were always willing to read, and my beta readers, writing mentors, and all-around incredible people who make my life better.

With love,

Aly

Thank you for reading this Feiwel & Friends book.

The friends who made

THE LAST UNEXPLORED
PLACE ON EARTH

possible are:

Jean Feiwel, Publisher

Liz Szabla, VP, Associate Publisher

Rich Deas, Senior Creative Director

Holly West, Senior Editor

Anna Roberto, Senior Editor

Kat Brzozowski, Senior Editor

Dawn Ryan, Executive Managing Editor

Kim Waymer, Senior Production Manager

Emily Settle, Editor

Rachel Diebel, Editor

Foyinsi Adegbonmire, Associate Editor

Brittany Groves, Assistant Editor

Julia Bianchi, Junior Designer

Lelia Mander, Production Editor

Follow us on Facebook or visit us online at

MACKIDS.COM.

Our books are friends for life.